THE CRAFT OF THE CLOCKMAKER

For Clive

THE CRAFT OF THE CLOCKMAKER

E.J.Tyler

CROWN
PUBLISHERS,
INC.
NEW YORK

ACKNOWLEDGEMENTS
The author and publishers would like to thank the
following for the use of photographs in this book:
British Museum, The Worshipful Company of
Clockmakers and the Guildhall Librarian, S.
Lanzetter & Co., Mr. Brian Pearson and the
Science Museum.
They would also like to thank Mr. K. D. Roberts
and Mr. Edward Ingraham for permission to
reproduce extracts from their catalogues and to
Mr. W. Fonteyn for the Blakeborough advertise-
ment.

First published in the United States by
Crown Publishers, Inc., 1974

Library of Congress Catalog Card Number: 74-80310

Designed by Conal Buck

Text filmset in 11/11½ pt Monophoto
Garamond 156 by Typesetting Services Ltd.,
Glasgow, Scotland

Printed and bound in the U.S.A.

CONTENTS

PREFACE

With the increasing interest that is being taken in antique clocks and watches many books appear on the subject of the clocks and watches themselves, but very little is written on how they have been made. The present work is an attempt to fill the gap and describe how the clock and watch-maker of the past carried on his business. It is not intended as a textbook on how to make or repair clocks and watches: the bibliography contains references to works of this nature.

The writer's thanks are due to many people for their assistance in his task and in particular to:
Mr. Beresford Hutchinson of the British Museum, Messrs. A. A. Osborne & Son Ltd. for the loan of tools for illustrations, Mr. R. J. Street for the loan of clocks for the illustrations and to Mrs. Phyllis Street for typing the manuscript.

1
THE FIRST CLOCKS

The mechanical clock, like so many other inventions, did not come into being without a great deal of work being done in other fields which appears to have only a remote connection with the matter in hand. To produce a workable clock, the primary requirement is a thorough knowledge of working in metal with the capability to make parts that fit each other, and to provide a frame of sufficient rigidity to carry the moving parts without undergoing distortion, for the clock must be sufficiently well made to work continuously without attention. A knowledge of mathematics is necessary to calculate the numbers of teeth in the wheels and a knowledge of astronomy is required to determine the standard to which the clock is intended to work.

As for the date of the earliest clock, it was probably made somewhere between 1270 and 1300. Dante writes in *Il Paradiso* before 1321 about a clock, so it had been invented before this. Milan claims to have had the first public clock in 1335.

MEDIEVAL IRONWORKING

No work can be done without proper tools, and the creation of such a machine needs a number of tools, some of which were already known, plus some specialised ones for specific uses, in particular files and turning tools. The leading technologists of the Middle Ages were the smiths, particularly those who had dealings with armour and weapons of war. The Middle Ages was the heyday of the smith in Britain. Small towns and villages would each have had their own, with a greater density in the larger towns. The smiths' best patrons at this time were ecclesiastical establishments. There was

Fireplace, 1st century B.C. An early example of a rectangular frame constructed in iron

a great demand for gates, railings, grilles and door hinges for all the numerous churches and monasteries. Many of these pieces have been preserved, such as the grille made for the tomb of Queen Eleanor of Castile in 1294, still to be seen in Westminster Abbey.

The decorative ironwork was most influenced by France and the Middle East via the Crusades. Blacksmiths going out as farriers or armourers were inspired by the work on oriental buildings and imitated it when they came home.

The iron of those days was prepared in the same primitive fashion that had been used for centuries. The ore was roasted to break it up and make it easier to smelt by converting the carbonate of iron into oxide and driving off the water content. It was then mixed with flux and heated in a clay furnace over charcoal which was kept burning brightly by means of bellows. The impurities mixed with the flux to form slag, and the mixture of iron and slag was removed from the furnace and hammered so that the slag would be driven out. The slag having a lower melting point than the iron was in a treacly condition at the temperature used. A lot of iron was wasted by this process, and the finished piece of iron or 'bloom' would still contain impurities which could only be removed by further hammering. It is important to note that the iron was never melted by this process. It merely became soft enough to allow the slag to be expelled by the hammers. Molten iron could only be produced by a blast furnace, the first of which was probably erected near Liège about 1400. The first in Britain was erected about 1500. By means of the blast furnace, a few hours' work could produce several hundredweight of iron as against several pounds by the old method, and the iron could be run into moulds to form castings. The product is called 'cast iron', and although very hard it is also brittle and less suitable for clock work than hammered or wrought iron.

The water-powered hammer was rare before 1500 but was most useful when dealing with large blooms of iron. Round about 1300, when we assume the clock first appeared, all iron would have been hammered by hand and would therefore have been expensive. It would also have been difficult to transport unless carried by water. Its purity could not be guaranteed, and it might suffer from an abundance of sulphur in which case it would be known as 'hot short' and would crumble or break instead of taking shape under the hammer when hot, or it might contain too much phosphorus, in which case it would be known as 'cold short' and would be weak or brittle when cold.

When iron is combined with small quantities of carbon it forms steel. Steel is stronger than iron and possesses the quality of becoming hard when heated to redness and then suddenly quenched in water or oil. In this condition it is to a certain extent brittle, but some of the hardness can be removed by subsequent gentle heating while the operator watches the colour of the oxide forming on the surface. The colour changes from a pale straw to a darker brown and then to blue and black. The various colours indicate degrees of hardness which are suitable for various purposes, e.g. the straw for cutting tools and the blue for finished parts of clocks and watches. Hardening and tempering is used a great deal in clock and watch work, the pieces being shaped while comparatively soft and then hardened to resist wear when performing their allotted task. Steel was difficult to make in the early days, and medieval clocks were made of wrought iron, which was comparatively easy to get, large quantities of it being made in Sussex from Roman times onwards.

THE EARLIEST CLOCKS

No one knows exactly how or where the mechanical clock came into being, but in view of the fact that the smiths of the day were extensively employed on work for the church one might infer the collaboration of a scientifically minded monk with a particularly skilled ironworker, who had probably served in the Crusades and brought back some ideas from the Arabs. All the work would have been done without the use of powered hammers. The smith then, like the clockmaker in later years, would have made practically all his own tools and would have been in a position to produce whatever special tools were needed. The earliest clocks were of large size; the reason for this being that the technology of the time would have been better adapted to make a large clock than a small one. Even today we find that the 'mini' version of an object appears after the full size one is well established.

The clock's main function in the earliest days was to strike the hours on a bell to inform the monks of the times of services, and a bell that could be heard over greater distances would be larger and need a correspondingly larger mechanism to strike it. Previously the monasteries had used water clocks which needed a human observer to ring the bell at the appropriate time. A mechanical clock would do away with the human watcher and strike automatically, which was a great improvement on the old system. The position that the clock would have occupied in the church is uncertain. Old manuscripts show clocks with very large movements placed at ground level with elaborately painted cases over them. This position would have carried on the tradition of the old water clocks, and the only advantage gained from putting the clock high up in the tower, would be to make the rope connecting with the bell hammer shorter and possibly to allow the weights to hang vertically beneath the clock. Exterior dials came later, although some of the early clocks at ground level were fitted with dials.

THE FIRST CLOCKMAKERS

As clocks came to be used more widely, there was not only a need for men to make them, but also for men to repair them. It is probable that the first clockmakers were itinerant, carrying their tools with them and moving on a regular circuit. The smallest groups would possibly have had two men and a boy and the largest possibly five all told. Their transport would have been by horses, and as the roads at that time were almost non-existent, it is probable that packhorses would have been preferred to carts. When a town was reached where a clock had to be made or repaired, the clockmakers would use the local blacksmith's forge by arrangement. We have evidence of this from the Churchwardens' accounts at Rye in the sixteenth century when repairs were needed to the church clock there. The Churchwardens not only paid for the use of the forge and coals, but also the clock-maker's board and lodging.

There is evidence that three Lombards, whose names are not recorded, were working for Edward III on a clock for Windsor Castle in 1352. He also granted a charter of protection to three 'orologiers' from Delft in 1368 who have been credited with the making of the clocks at Salisbury and Wells. Dr. C. F. C. Beeson has recently investigated the records of the making of a clock at Perpignan in 1356 which brought together a number of craftsmen, not only concerned with the actual clock itself, but also men connected with the masonry, carpentry and other trades. They even erected a special forge for the clock-makers to work at. The Exeter Cathedral records show that Roger the clockmaker was fetched from Barnstaple in 1424 to repair the clock. It is unlikely that Barnstaple would have been his home, as such a craftsman would have been based on a city like Exeter. He may have been working at Barnstaple at the time on one of his journeys round the country.

An early Turret clock with verge escapement and foliot balance from Cassiobury Park, Hertfordshire

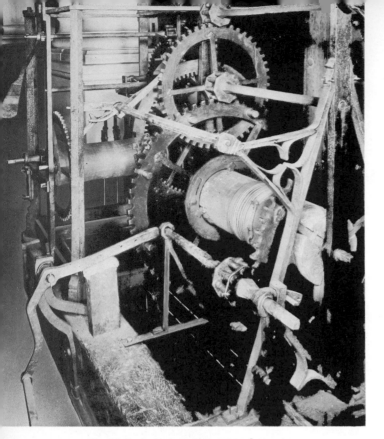

The Wells Cathedral clock (1392) showing how the ends of the crossings embrace the wheeldrum, the octagonal arbors and lantern pinions

CLOCK FRAMES

A precedent for the shape of the frames of early clocks is found in the British Museum, where a fireplace built up of iron bars with decorated finials is displayed. This came from Welwyn and dates from the first century B.C. No doubt similar ones were in use in other parts of Europe.

The chief requirement of a clock frame is that it must be rigid enough to resist any twisting movements caused by the pull of the weights which would cause the pivots to be gripped in their holes. These holes must be placed accurately opposite each other so that the 'arbor' or spindle runs true in relation to the frame, and so that the holes can be kept to the minimum size and not have to be opened out to allow for a slight misalignment of the arbors. All the parts of a medieval clock were beaten out of the rough iron and then finished

with files. Slots in the frames were cut out with a chisel and hammer after the position of the slot had been marked with a punch, and the tongues of the members fitting into the slots were beaten out on the anvil and finished with a file to make a good fit. Another slot was cut in the tongue to receive the wedge which held the part in position, and as soon as all the parts of the frame were made, they were fastened together and the whole arrangement tested for squareness and rigidity. Once a satisfactory fit had been obtained, the wedges were driven tight and the holes for the pivots marked.

The easiest way to tackle this job was to make the wheels, mount them on their arbors together with their pinions and find by experiment the 'depths' or distances apart that the arbors would have to be placed. When the positions of these holes had been determined, they could be marked by chalk and the holes drilled. The blacksmith's way of making a hole by heating the metal red hot and then piercing the bar with a punch, followed by a tapered drift to open the hole to the correct size, could not be used here because re-heating and working the iron would upset the careful measurements just made. Drilling cold was necessary here.

MAKING CLOCK PARTS

The making of the wheels themselves was similar to the making of horseshoes, in that a bar was bent into a curve and then flattened on its side. In the case of the wheel, however, the ends of the bar were welded to form a circle, and then this was flattened into an annular shape. The 'crossings' or spokes often have a trefoil at the ends to grasp the wheel rim. This trefoil is slotted so that the rim fits into the slot and the rim itself is also slotted so that the crossing has something to bear against as it turns. The part of the arbor where the wheel seating is formed, is square or octagonal and the ends of the crossings are forked in the centre and welded into a boss so that the wheel is rigidly fixed to the arbor.

The cutting of the teeth was probably done before mounting, although the wheel may have been fitted to its arbor and removed again after circles had been marked on the rim to indicate the tips and bases of the teeth. The teeth would have been cut by hand after marking out and the tips rounded as a separate operation. Pinions were made in the lantern form, i.e. two discs or octagons of sheet metal separated by a number of short rods which are placed in a circle, and are driven by the wheel on the adjacent arbor. This form is easier to make than the solid form and is also more tolerant of inaccurate depths, but this does not preclude the early use of a solid pinion by someone who was skilful with a file.

After the arbors had been inserted in the frame, it was necessary to rotate them slowly to find any places where the meshing was inaccurate and after that apply the necessary corrections. Tooth cutting had to be done very carefully as inaccurate work involved the making of a new wheel and the loss of many hours of labour. If we consider the clock now exhibited in Salisbury Cathedral as a medieval clock reduced to its basic components, the cutting of the teeth involved three ordinary wheels and the scapewheel plus the count wheel which has internal teeth on its rim and the graduated slots for controlling the number of blows struck on its outer edge.

The octagonal shape of the arbors of medieval clocks is due to the fact that they were finished by the hammer and not turned, except possibly the pivots. There was probably some primitive form of turning between dead centres to finish the latter. However, as the diameter of the piece increases so does the necessity for a stronger support for the work being turned and also a greater driving force to rotate it, hence the reluctance to do any more turning than was absolutely necessary.

The bars of medieval turret clocks are generally parallel throughout their length. In later clocks the bars are often widened where the pivots come, this being accomplished by heating the iron locally and hitting the end of the bar on the anvil or 'upsetting' it.

It could not have been long after the invention of the clock that attempts were made to reduce its size. The oldest wall clock in the world is claimed to be the one in the Main–Frankisches Museum at Wurzburg with a suggested date of 1352. This clock consists of a main wheel and scapewheel with another wheel carrying the hour hand, which is driven off a pinion on the main arbor. Primitive alarm work driven by a crank is also included. There is no striking mechanism.

Locksmiths were also at work in the Middle Ages. They worked with the metal cold, but obtained it from the same source as the blacksmiths, the difference being that it was beaten out into smaller pieces before the work began. Their most important tool was the file and each locksmith must have possessed a good stock of them. The earliest small clocks must have been made by men trained as locksmiths, but some of the frames of these clocks show signs of blacksmiths' work as well in certain parts, although on a much smaller scale than on the turret clocks.

EARLY DOMESTIC CLOCKS

The earliest clocks intended for domestic use are known as Gothic wall clocks or chamber clocks. Their movements are much taller in proportion than the turret clocks as they have an additional wheel in each train to limit the fall of the weights. The principle of the mechanism is the same, but the balance in many of these clocks is in the form of a wheel instead of the bar or 'foliot' of the older clocks. Regulation of the earlier clocks was achieved by moving the weights at the end of the foliot further from or nearer to the centre, but clocks with a wheel balance had to have the driving weight altered, so the top of the weight was made cup-shaped so lead shot could be added or removed for the purpose.

THE MAINSPRING

A further development in the construction of the clock was the use of a mainspring for motive power instead of the weights, thereby rendering the clock portable. The earliest spring clocks resembled the wall clocks in appearance, if we accept the evidence of a painting by Rogier van der Weyden in the Museum of Fine Arts at Antwerp. The picture was painted about 1470 and shows a Burgundian nobleman with a small clock hanging near him, apparently the springs of this clock are located in the base. The spring clock soon developed a style of its own with two main types; the one being like a small tower with a vertical dial on the side, while the other was lower with the dial on the top. These clocks usually had gold or gilt cases which were elaborately engraved, but the movements were still made of iron and were quite rough.

As a spring exerts more force when it is fully wound and gradually loses power as it runs down, some compensation device is necessary to provide an even pull during the period that the clock is running. Nowadays springs can be made much longer, which causes less variation in the driving force, and with modern escapements the problem is less acute. With the verge escapement controlled by a foliot or wheel balance, variations in

power cause a variation in timekeeping. The usual method of compensating for variations in the driving force was by means of the 'fusee'. A fusee is a tapered piece of metal shaped roughly like a cone which spreads out a little wider at its base. A spiral groove is cut round the fusee to receive a gut line, the other end of which is fastened to a drum called the 'barrel' which contains the mainspring. To wind the clock, the fusee is rotated, thereby drawing the gut line into the groove and rotating the barrel, which causes the spring to be wound. The line is so arranged that when the spring is fully wound the pull is on the small diameter of the fusee, and as the spring gets weaker the diameter of the groove increases and provides a more or less constant torque throughout the running period.

Making a mainspring must have been an extremely difficult task in the Middle Ages. Every piece of steel would have possessed unpredictable qualities, and faults that were not apparent during the course of manufacture would only have revealed themselves after the clock had been assembled. Many hours of work would thereby have been rendered useless. The steel strip had to be very smooth, free from cracks and as near as possible the same thickness throughout its length. It had to be hardened and accurately tempered using the same skills as were needed by armourers or sword makers, and once again the connection between these trades and the mechanical clock comes to the fore.

The creation of the steel itself from iron was a complicated process, involving much hammering and reheating to get the iron to absorb the right amount of carbon. In view of the difficulties of making springs, it may well have been necessary to make four or five before getting one that was acceptable and the cost of the clock would therefore be greatly increased. The possessors of the earliest spring clocks must have been men of great wealth such as kings or noblemen connected with the court.

A clock movement with a fusee showing the gut line partly on the fusee and partly on the barrel which contains the mainspring. The ratchet at the front is for putting tension on the spring before the clock is wound

2
THE SIXTEENTH AND SEVENTEENTH CENTURIES

When they started making domestic clocks, we find that the clockmakers began to have a fixed address. Another change that appeared, was the use of solid pinions which need skill in the use of a file for their making. Documentary evidence of how clockmakers worked on these clocks in the fourteenth and fifteenth centuries is scanty, but we have several interesting illustrations to consider.

About 1470 there was produced a woodcut called *The Children of Mercury* which included a clockmaker at his work. He is adjusting a weight-driven chamber clock, and on the bench beside him are a spare toothed wheel and a foliot and verge. An old illustration of about 1480 shows a clockmaker sighting a heavenly body by means of a quadrant, presumably to obtain the time. A Gothic chamber clock is standing on the bench beside him with one of the wheels lying near it, so he cannot be attempting to regulate this clock. Among the tools present are a hammer and what is presumably a file.

THE AMMAN WOODCUT

A woodcut by Jost Amman, illustrating a work of Hans Sachs dating from 1568, shows an open shop front with a counter before it. Two men are working at the counter and one of them, presumably the master, is assembling a Gothic chamber clock with a moon dial above it. It is easy to see inside the shop; this was done in order to admit the maximum amount of light, and also to reveal that no other trades than that controlled by the master's Guild were carried on there. While the work in hand is a chamber clock, a very large wheel on the counter suggests that turret clocks may also have been made in this establishment. There is a forge in the background and a workman is beating out what looks like a dial for another chamber clock. On the counter are some wheels and a foliot and verge.

THE STRADANUS PRINT

The well known print by Stradanus of Antwerp, *Horologia Ferrea* gives us an even better picture of the workshop of a contemporary clockmaker. The shop appears to

The Amman woodcut

deal with all types of clock from spring-driven table clocks to turret clocks, to say nothing of the 'Nuremberg Egg' type of watch. At the rear of the shop is a forge with a tank of water beside it, a smith is holding a piece of work in the fire with a long pair of tongs while another man works the bellows. A Gothic chamber clock hangs on the wall beside the forge while yet another man is examining a rack from which hang a number of watches. Before the forge stands an anvil with a hammer lying on it and at its base are supported another lighter hammer and a pair of pincers, while another pair lies on the floor.

There is a certain feeling that the picture has been deliberately composed rather than depicting a definite scene, because the man who is heating the metal would have a long walk to the anvil wasting precious seconds while his piece of iron was cooling. Two of the persons present appear to be left-handed, the man on the extreme left who is filing out a wheel and the customer in the foreground who wears his sword on his right and his dagger on his left-hand side. The man at the bench is working beside the master, who is also engaged in wheel making and has just removed a wheel from the vice to examine the teeth. Beside him is the frame of a table clock movement and the elaborate case is also present. The workman also appears to be working on a table clock, but one less elaborate than that of the master. They each have a selection of files on the bench, similar files to those in use today

The Stradanus print

HOROLOGIA FERREA.

Ioan. Stradanus invent.   *Phls Galle excud.*

Rota æqua ferrea ætherisq̃ voluitur,   Recludit æquè et hæc et illa tempora.

except that the end is knobbed. The action of filing is interesting as the file appears to be pushed with the palm of the hand, the outer end being guided by the other hand, instead of using the grip that would be taken with a wooden handle. The men are working from drawings, and beside the master on the bench is a little portable clock or watch with its ribbon and the outer covering case.

The foreground is occupied by a large clock, probably intended for a very large room. A similar clock is displayed in the British Museum and the size is equal to that of a contemporary turret clock. The customer has come to inspect the clock while it is being worked upon, and the foliot for it is standing against the master's bench. The artist has drawn it upside down, and has shown both the visible wheels as 'contrate wheels', i.e. with the teeth parallel to the arbor. A large wheel and a hammer lying on the floor are probably put in for the sake of composition.

Standing beside the bench are the frame and some wheels for a Gothic chamber clock. Three of these clocks are in the shop undergoing trials, and the fact that the heap of parts includes the rim of a wheel balance suggests that these clocks have wheel balances as well instead of being fitted with a foliot. There is a suggestion of this in the way the clocks are drawn, and the fact that the clocks possess more box-like cases than most of the early chamber clocks makes it more probable, as there would be difficulty in adjusting the weights on the foliot for regulation with this type of case.

One or two wheels hanging on the wall are probably there to give atmosphere, as it is unlikely that wheels would be kept in stock at this early period. No more wheels would be made than was absolutely necessary for the clocks under construction, at any given time. The clocks have weights with counterpoises, hence they are fitted for cords instead of chains. The men are wearing short aprons, possibly of leather, and all are wearing hats. The thickness of the bench top should be noticed. It is probably as much as $3\frac{1}{2}$ inches thick and makes a very firm support for the vices, which would need to be kept absolutely rigid for the accurate filing of the wheel teeth.

A large Chamber clock similar to the one in the Stradanus print

The woodturner's lathe

TURNING

It is unfortunate that no turning is being shown. This operation is one of the most fascinating carried out in a workshop and is also extremely important. Turning has been known for many centuries and in the Middle Ages the commonest form would have been wood turning. The primitive apparatus used by wood turners consists of two horizontal metal prongs which can be fixed at varying distances apart to accommodate the work, an adjustable rest to support the tool and the cord which gives the work a rotary motion. This is fastened to a pedal beneath the bench and is held in tension by a sapling placed above which has its other end securely anchored. One turn of the cord is put round the work, in such a way that pressure on the pedal rotates the work with the top surface coming towards the operator. When the pedal has completed its stroke, pressure is released and the sapling returns the pedal to its former position. Continuous rotation is not achieved but there is sufficient time to make a cut during the down stroke and the tool then has to be moved away slightly as the work rotates in the opposite direction. An expert with such a lathe can make a chair leg in about one and a half minutes

A similar apparatus on a smaller scale was used by watch and clockmakers for turning, but naturally there were differences. The horologist's lathe was usually known as a 'turns' and was very accurately made with a number of accessories for performing specialised operations. The drive was provided by a bow which was operated by the worker's left hand while he held the tool with his right. Instead of the bowstring being wrapped round the work itself as was usual in wood turning, the clockmaker used ferrules which could be easily applied to and removed from the piece being worked on and which possessed a smooth pulley which would rotate the work evenly without chafing the cord. The to-and-fro motion was retained, but it is possible that by the seventeenth century some makers had obtained a continuous rotary motion through the use of a hand-driven flywheel mounted behind the turns. Such an apparatus is generally known as a 'throw' and it greatly speeds the work. Very large wheels to provide continuous rotation were used in the seventeenth century in the diamond polishing industry, and the homely spinning wheel also forms an example of its application. Although the principle was illustrated by Leonardo da Vinci, the horological trade seems reluctant to have adopted it and the to-and-fro motion is still in use today for some operations as it gives very sensitive speed control and the opportunity to examine the work after each cut.

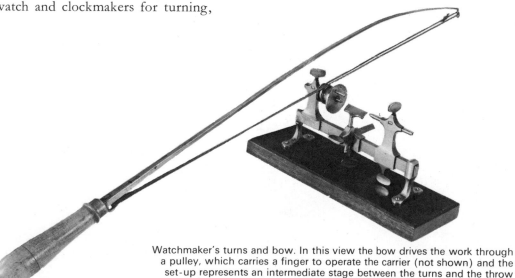

Watchmaker's turns and bow. In this view the bow drives the work through a pulley, which carries a finger to operate the carrier (not shown) and the set-up represents an intermediate stage between the turns and the throw

HOROLOGICAL TOOLS

One of the most important documents in the history of horological tools is an inventory of the equipment of a watch-maker in Leeuwarden, Friesland, which was made on the occasion of his marriage in 1600. The inventory is reproduced in *Geschiedenis van de Uurwerkmakerskunst in Friesland* by Nanne Ottema, and a few details concerning the man himself, whose name was Wijbe Vibrandi can be found in *De Leeuwarder Uurwerkmakers en hun werk in het Fries Museum* by J. H. Leopold. Vibrandi had worked in Emden at one time and would therefore have been brought into contact with German technicians. It is more than likely that a lot of his equipment had been made by himself, including the files as the list includes file chisels. The making of a file was a highly skilled operation, although an experienced worker was able to cut the teeth with a hammer and chisel very rapidly and afterwards the metal was hardened and tempered. The very small files used for watches and clocks were naturally more difficult to make than the larger sizes.

Files form a very important part of the inventory. The first item in this category is a file for finishing springs, so Vibrandi was skilled in this part of the work also. Next are six fine files with handles and brass rings (to keep the handles from splitting) and twelve coarse ones the same. There are thirty-two small, fine files with handles (not like those in the Stradanus illustration), eight small files with handles and rings as above, fifteen Nuremberg files, forty small Nuremberg files and thirty small steel files with 'eyes' behind, presumably like those in the Stradanus illustration with no wooden handles. There follow ten steel files 'flat at the back'. This could mean having cutting edges on one face only, as in the files used for rounding up the teeth of wheels. Then come another half dozen small files, two dozen 'wire' files (possibly rat-tail files), three dozen piercing files and twenty-eight needle files. Altogether there are 248

A clockmaker's throw; large size for turret clocks

files. There are also large and small anvils with the necessary hammers and a double bellows for dealing with forging, several turns and the necessary turning tools and a bench with two drawers under it. A brass pan for blueing steel, casting flasks and a borax bath (for hard soldering) give an indication of other processes carried out with the aid of heat. Dividers and rulers are used for marking out and a division plate is used for marking the numbers of the teeth in the wheels. This would have been a brass plate with concentric circles engraved on it, each circle containing a certain number of equidistant holes. Later in the century the division plate was combined with a rotary file for cutting wheels accurately and rapidly, but in 1600 it would have been used for marking out only, and the workman would have cut each space with a file by hand. Shears for cutting metal together with tongs, engraving tools, drills, broaches for enlarging holes, soldering irons and various pots for holding molten metal complete the list. Materials include six mainsprings, some bells, a supply of brass and one or two clocks and watches. Also included in the inventory are some religious books and other items which do not concern the workshop.

A CLOCKMAKER'S SKILLS

The above will show the number of operations in which a clockmaker had to be skilled. He worked with sheet metal and castings, and did turning, forging, soldering and engraving. He even made his own bells and files as well as many other of the tools he needed. It specifically mentions at the beginning of the inventory that Vibrandi made watches of brass. Brass first came into use for watches and clocks about 1560. It is softer than iron and cannot be hardened by heating and quenching. The only way of hardening it is by 'working', i.e. drawing it into wire, rolling it or hammering it. Most clocks and watches have brass wheels and steel pinions. By this means, friction is reduced, because two surfaces made of dissimilar metals suffer less friction when rubbing over each other than if they are made of the same metal. Steel is chosen for the pinions because they have to stand much more wear than

A clockmaker's throw; normal size for domestic clocks

the wheels, but as dirt can get between the teeth and the leaves it embeds itself in the softer brass and acts as a cutting medium on the steel pinion, causing the leaves to wear after a time while the teeth on the brass wheel appear to be untouched.

The introduction of brass into horology took place on the Continent, but did not immediately spread to England because there was no native brass industry. The government were trying to foster the industry in the 1560s and invited Germans to come over to work mines and supply the necessary technology for working on the finished product. An Augsburg firm invested heavily in the project and sent a man over to take charge of operations. Forty or fifty miners came from the Tyrol in 1565 to develop copper mines in Cumberland and in 1566, calamine or zinc carbonate was discovered in Somerset. The necessary materials were now to hand and the manufacture of brass began, although it was inferior to the foreign product for about another century. Two Royal Companies were incorporated for the purposes of mining and manufacture.

16th CENTURY ENGLAND

It is highly probable that all or most of the clockmakers working in Britain before the end of the Elizabethan era, were foreigners. As late as 1540 when Henry VIII was building Nonsuch Palace, a group of French clockmakers were working on a clock there. Rye church clock was repaired in 1533 by 'a Frenchman' of unknown name. The earliest clocks made by clockmakers with an established address in London show French influence. We do not find records of men with English sounding names until the very end of the sixteenth century. The Elizabethan era was important because the government attempted to build up industries in Britain which were formerly Continental monopolies, and in particular established mines and workshops for dealing with metal. Hundreds of religious refugees were admitted to the country, some of whom helped in the expansion of the textile industry, and no doubt clockmakers were also included in their number. It is noteworthy that some of the technical terms used in horology are of French origin, e.g. Barrel is derived from *barrilet* and fusee from *fusée*—a distaff full of thread.

Clocks existing in Britain at this time were Gothic wall clocks with iron movements, spring-driven table clocks with iron or brass movements and the large iron turret clocks found in many church towers up and down the country. Practically all of them would have been made by foreigners, the few exceptions being turret clocks which were larger and therefore easier to make, and constructed by techniques already known to the thriving body of blacksmiths in the country. The turret clocks were easy to maintain, being often looked after by the sexton, and would not require much attention beyond winding and lubrication. Any new parts required could generally be supplied by the local blacksmith and the chief replacements needed were ropes, which had to be renewed every two or three years. Lubrication was usually by 'oyle' according to churchwardens' accounts and this was probably whale oil. Sometimes 'Sallet oyle' (olive oil) was used, and it has been known for 'Goose Likker' to be employed.

Clocks in towers in damp places would have suffered from the effects of the moisture, and rust would form on the movements in patches where the iron had absorbed sufficient carbon to become steel. There is a record in the Churchwardens' accounts in 1556 of Rye (Sussex), of the purchase of 'hair cloth for the windows where the clock hangeth' which probably refers to this. The generally dirty conditions found in church towers would result in the movement quickly becoming dirty, and the generous application of lubrication to all parts would result in a grinding paste which helped to shorten their life. This was where the blacksmith came in. He could renew the lantern pinions and parts like the pallets which underwent a great deal of wear, while if a visiting clockmaker were required, it was usually arranged for him to use the blacksmith's forge for any work he wanted to do.

REPAIRING DOMESTIC CLOCKS

The domestic clocks had to be attended to by a proper clockmaker. Their exposed movements would need frequent cleaning, and the cords bearing the weights would also fray and need replacing. New parts to replace those which had been worn would require the use of a vice, files and probably a turns. The spring-driven table clocks would also have to be maintained by an expert. They would be less exposed than a Gothic wall clock and therefore less liable to get dirty, but deterioration of the animal or vegetable lubricants used would retard the motion of the wheels and possibly cause chemical action to take place on the metal. The most sensitive part of the clock was the mainspring, and the gut line was also susceptible to wear and needed frequent renewal. The early springs were short and very strong and consequently put a great tension on the line. A breaking line would whip round like a flail and probably break a pivot or two, involving all the labour of making pinions and mounting the wheels from the old pinions on to them. If the clock were dropped, the shock might break the verge which would have to be remade and the balance re-mounted.

Other potential sources of danger are suggested by paintings from seventeenth century Holland. In Apsley House there is a painting by Jan Steen called *The Dissolute Household* where a monkey is playing with the cords of a wall clock, reminding us that pet monkeys were not uncommon in wealthy houses in the days gone by. The numerous naughty children that this artist portrays in various pictures suggest a further danger for contemporary clocks.

When we come to consider watches, the same problems existed as for table clocks, but in a more acute form. The breaking of the line would do as much damage to the arbors and pivots and might even cause one or two teeth to be broken. The problem of lubrication would also be as serious as in the larger time-keepers.

THE FUSEE

The use of a fusee also created another general problem which had to be overcome. When all the line has been wound off the fusee on to the barrel, no more power is applied to the train and the watch or clock stops. However, there must still be some tension on the line otherwise it would slacken and get tangled, preventing it being rewound tidily. This is accomplished by having a separate ratchet fixed to the barrel arbor, quite distinct from the ratchet in the fusee that allows re-winding. The barrel ratchet is held by a click fastened to the frame and remains stationary while the clock or watch is going. After all the wheels have been put in position and the plates have been firmly pinned together, the line is quite loose and the barrel ratchet is disengaged. When the barrel arbor is rotated, it pulls on the spring and so rotates the barrel. By steadily rotating the barrel by means of the arbor, the line can be wound on to the barrel, and it is guided on and held firm by the left hand. When all the line is on the barrel and the point of attachment to the fusee is in such a position that the latter cannot rotate, the barrel arbor is given an extra half turn or so and then the ratchet is secured by the click, which is firmly fastened in place. The necessary tension is then on the line.

In theory, the force acting upon the train is the same throughout the period of going, so by increasing the 'set up' of the spring a stronger pull can be obtained throughout the going period, and by decreasing it the opposite effect is obtained. In the days before the balance spring, adjusting mainspring tension was the main method of regulating a watch, and the watch would need to go to the watchmaker to have the tension adjusted if it were running fast or slow. Later watches have a worm operated by a key to set up the mainspring so that the owner could make any adjustments himself, and this feature was found even after the balance spring had become well established.

In order to prevent overwinding, fusees are fitted with a stopwork. This usually consists of a hinged lever fitted to the top plate of the clock or watch and kept in position by a flat spring. As the last turn of the line comes on to the fusee, it pushes this lever into the way of a beak fitted to the fusee and so stops winding. There is usually a quarter of a turn of line left on the barrel when the watch or clock is fully wound, and if this were wound on to the fusee after the grooves were full it might wrap itself round the arbor and prevent the fusee from rotating.

Fusees of very old clocks and watches are thinner than later ones and have less difference between their largest and smallest diameters. They must have been extremely difficult to make by hand and the engines for producing them that were used in the eighteenth century, are unlikely to have been used in the fifteenth or sixteenth. The marking would probably have been done with the fusee blank mounted in a turns and a tool moved along the rest while the fusee was slowly rotated. A very steady hand and accurate eye would be needed.

THE 17th CENTURY

By the early seventeenth century, clock and watch-making had become an established trade in London even if the work were performed by foreigners or men of foreign descent. It was not long before native talent had developed and the clockmakers of London were petitioning the King for incorporation in order to restrict the employment of foreigners in the trade. The charter for the Clockmakers' Company was not granted till 1631 which was comparatively late. Paris clockmakers had been incorporated in 1544 and various continental cities had their guilds before London did.

It was in the early seventeenth century that the first typically English clock made its appearance, the type that is now generally known as a lantern clock. It was basically the Gothic type of wall clock controlled by a balance, with brass wheels instead of iron ones and a case and dial of polished brass replacing the continental sheet iron case and dial, which was often decorated with painting. The layout of the movement was the same as before and it was only in the use of brass for the decoration and the wheels that the new design differed. Maintenance problems were little different from those of the European style of wall clock, and the chief advantage would lie in the fact that brass is easier to work with than iron.

By this time, British craftsmen had mastered the art of making watches also. Makers such as John Midnall, Richard Crayle, Robert Grinkin and Simon Bartram were making watches of small size with beautifully cut teeth on their brass wheels. The decoration of the movements with filigree and engraving that was so prominent from the late seventeenth to the early nineteenth centuries, had already begun but on a less elaborate scale.

One of the features of the Clockmakers' Company's policy was the restriction of the number of apprentices that a clockmaker could have. He could only take one with the consent of the Master of the Company until he himself became a senior official of the Company, after which he might have two but never more. After the first apprentice had served five years, another could be taken, but not sooner, under a penalty of ten pounds. The motive appears to have been to maintain a shortage of skilled labour to keep prices up,

Movement of an English Lantern clock with wheel balance

but several eminent members of the craft disobeyed the regulation in the early days and were fined. Business was brisk and they wanted to make the most of it.

The Restoration period was a time of change in the horological trade. Christian Huygens had applied the pendulum to clockwork in Holland, and pendulum clocks were being made in London by the Fromanteel family as early as 1658. After the Restoration, people were anxious to shake off the austerity of the Commonwealth period and among the new furnishings for their homes that they ordered were clocks made with the new controller. The earliest pendulum clocks in Holland were spring-driven and dispensed with fusees, although it was scarcely ever omitted from British examples. They were a development of the spring-driven table clocks previously used, although it was not long before weight-driven versions were being made. These weight clocks had more in common with the table clocks, as far as their movements were concerned, than with the Gothic wall clocks previously produced. They had very large main wheels and barrels, but the rest of the wheelwork was very small and delicate. This persisted after the invention of the anchor escapement about 1670 but in later years there was not such a contrast in the sizes of the wheels.

APPLICATION OF THE PENDULUM

Huygens' discovery made the clocks so much more accurate that it was now worth while to fit a minute hand. This involved the addition of extra wheels behind the dial, but meant that the striking could be discharged by a pin on a wheel which rotated once per hour, instead of a twelve pointed star which rotated once in twelve hours. The single hour hand required a fair amount of force to move it when the clock was being set to time and consequently was made very strong, but it required much less force to alter a clock by means of the minute hand, and consequently the design for these could be made much lighter and lead to new possibilities in decoration. Some very fine designs in hands were produced in the late seventeenth century and can be seen on clocks by such makers as Christopher Gould. By this time, hand making had become a specialised trade distinct from that of clockmaking.

The advent of clocks that told time to a greater degree of accuracy than before, created a demand for old clocks to be converted to the new method. Many lantern clocks are extant showing signs of conversion, either by having an additional contrate wheel i.e. a wheel which has its teeth set at right angles to its plane, added which drives a small verge scapewheel on top of the clock controlled by a short 'bob' pendulum, or having an anchor escapement with long pendulum. When a clock has been converted, the old holes are generally left behind and supply the evidence that the clock was formerly balance controlled. The anchor scapewheel arbor is often supported by the cock that formerly carried the pivot of the verge scapewheel and allowed the verge to pass behind it. During the late seventeenth and early eighteenth centuries, many turret clocks were converted also and usually show some signs of their former escapement. All this work would involve the clockmakers in calculations and making of parts that they had not undertaken previously.

Huygens also applied the balance spring to watches, making them more accurate and therefore worthy of a minute hand. The English scientist, Robert Hooke, had the same idea at the same time and had a watch made by the celebrated maker, Thomas Tompion, which was presented to Charles II. The use of the balance spring not only involved the extra wheels behind the dial to allow for the minute hand, but also needed a regulator to be added whereby the effective length of the spring could be altered at will to change the rate of the watch. The old method of watch regulation was to increase or decrease the setting up of the mainspring, and often a small disc with numbers would be fitted to show the extent to which this had been done. The new method used a similar disc with a square at its centre which could be turned by a watch key and which operated a pinion gearing with a sector which carried two pins (the curb pins). These pins embraced the spring, and adjustment of the disc moved them nearer to or further from the point where the spring was fastened to the plate, thereby lengthening or shortening the effective portion of the spring and making the watch go slower or faster. The horologist now had to make the delicate balance spring as well. This operation involved flattening a fine wire and coiling it, polishing and tempering it and then fixing it in a collet to find by experiment the correct position for pinning it in its stud. The usual method of pinning is to thread the spring through a circular hole and fasten it with a circular tapered brass pin pushed in tight, but Tompion added the refinement of making the hole square and so doing away with the distortion that would occur when a flat spring was compressed against the side of a round hole.

Watch movement without balance spring, signed *Ri: Masterson The Exchange, Fecit.* 1st half of the 17th century

Watch movement with an early use of a balance spring, *Jacobus Markwick, London.* The spring is anchored near the foot of the balance cock and the end is straight. The curb pins which control the effective length, move along the straight section, their position is altered by turning the arbor near the edge of the plate, a pointer on a scale shows the amount moved

THOMAS TOMPION

Tompion himself created a revolution in clock and watch-making. About 6,000 pieces by him are known and, when we consider the number that must have been destroyed in the intervening three hundred years, it becomes apparent that no one man could have made so many pieces in his lifetime. He must have had a factory somewhere producing rough movements which were finished to each customer's requirements. By the eighteenth century, specialist workshops were supplying movements to the leading London makers and it is possible that Tompion may have been the pioneer of this practice, although there is as yet no evidence that any contemporary pieces bearing the name of other makers originated in his factory. An interesting proof of quantity production at this period is found in the Guildhall Museum. The collection includes six watch movements of about 1670, all alike and unfinished.

Tompion has been the subject of a biography, but there are still many things which we should like to know about him. He was born in 1638 in Northill in Bedfordshire, and is believed to have been apprenticed to the blacksmith's trade, later becoming a maker of 'great' i.e. turret, clocks. He came to London sometime after 1660 and was established as a clockmaker in Water Lane, Blackfriars in the early 1670s. He probably did not make watches at the beginning. His reputation was founded on good design of the parts of his timekeepers together with precision workmanship and he has become known as the Father of English Clockmaking. He was honoured by being buried in Westminster Abbey. Tompion was engaged upon work for Hooke in the early days but Hooke's diary records that they were not always on amiable terms.

It was during the later seventeenth century that the old type of open shop changed over to the closed type with which we are familiar today. An open window looking on to the street is hardly the place to sell watches, one needs a counter on which to display them and prevent their being accidentally dropped, chairs for the customers and freedom from draughts which blow in dust. The Stradanus illustration shows some watches hanging on the wall, but with the dust produced from the filing, the wind blowing in from the street and the smoke from the forge, it is not exactly an ideal spot for making or displaying them.

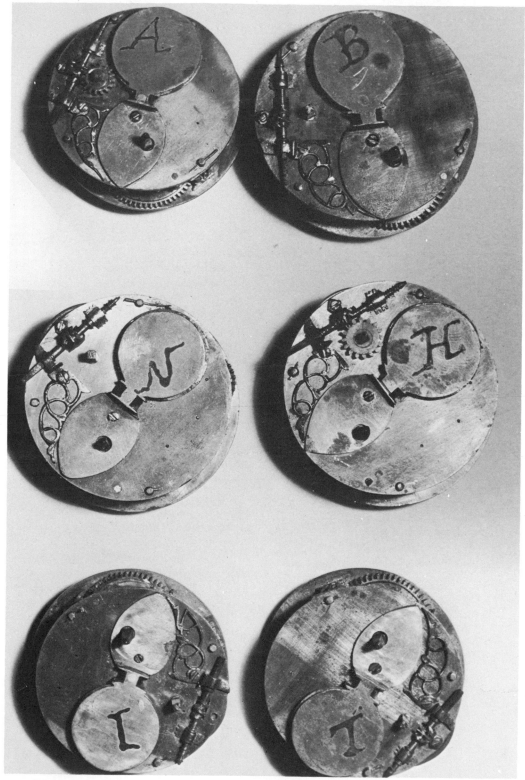

Six unfinished watch movements, about 1670. They are all alike and show
that bulk production was being carried out even at this early date

A typical mid-18th century English Bracket clock.
Hall, London

3 THE LONG-CASE CLOCK

In the last chapter it was seen that after the Restoration, clock and watch production increased and the trade was given an impetus by new inventions such as the pendulum, the balance spring and the anchor escapement. During the remaining years of the seventeenth century the eight-day long-case clock and the spring-driven pendulum clock, which is usually known as a 'Bracket Clock' although it was generally stood on a table in those days, became firmly established as the standard British timekeepers. The lantern clock became less popular with London makers and was often given a square dial and encased in a hood with the weight and pendulum exposed beneath it. With the country makers, the lantern clock remained in production and in the eighteenth century was often housed in a long-case with a square dial more reminiscent of its eight-day counterpart. We therefore have three basic movements in production which changed only in detail as the century progressed and were still being made up to the middle of the nineteenth century and in some cases even later. The spring-driven clock had a fusee for each train and was generally fitted with a verge escapement which was more tolerant to changes of position. This allowed the clock to run when 'out of beat' and so make it more portable. For this reason, these clocks usually had carrying handles until the late eighteenth century when the verge escapement gave way to the anchor.

The standard watch movement was very thick. It had the verge escapement and a highly decorated balance cock, while the balance spring only possessed a few turns. The top plate was further decorated by filigree work or engraving and the pillars were of an Egyptian or other decorated style. This type of movement persisted until well into the nineteenth century, becoming progressively plainer, until the last made were almost entirely devoid of decoration and had plain turned pillars. As new escapements were invented during the eighteenth and early nineteenth centuries, the movements were modified to receive them, but the basic layout underwent very little change.

MAKING A LONG-CASE CLOCK

Let us imagine we are watching a clockmaker make a long-case clock movement in the early eighteenth century. Later on there was a tendency to get movements wholly or partly finished from specialist workshops, but then there were still quite a number made by individual craftsmen. Our clockmaker may even at this early stage have got a number of pieces from specialised workers. The dials would also have been engraved by specialists and the cases made by local furniture makers.

The movement is made from two brass plates about 7 in. by 5 in. and $\frac{3}{16}$ in. thick, connected by four or more brass pillars. These pillars are turned ornamentally and have thick portions in the middle. The bottom two are pierced and threaded to take the screws which hold the movement to its seat board. The plates are cut from sheets of brass and have to be hammered all over to harden them and provide a sufficiently hard surface to act as bearings for the pivots. Some makers get over this problem by drilling the holes large and inserting hardened bushes, but in this case the plates themselves are to carry the pivot holes and so they are hammered or 'planished' all over and shaved smooth afterwards, the hammering has to be done evenly and not too hard, covering the whole surface. The hammer is specially made with a rounded face so as not to leave bruises on the metal. Some makers leave the front plate of the movement rough as it is not seen, being close behind the dial, and the rough surface is convenient for setting out the position of the trains.

The numbers of teeth in the wheels and the layout of the various parts are obtained from a book which the clockmaker has compiled during the years that he has been active. If he has succeeded to the business of an older man (e.g. the apprentice who married the master's daughter) he will probably go on using his master's designs. The book will be guarded very carefully as the secrets of the craft are closely maintained among its members.

Parts of an English Long-Case movement, early 18th century

CUTTING TEETH ON A WHEEL

The most arduous job in the making of a clock or watch movement is the cutting of the teeth of the wheels. These teeth must not only be accurately spaced, but must also possess a certain shape to make the engaging and disengaging with the pinion take place with the minimum of friction. Their edges must be smoothed and polished and they must be strong enough to resist the driving force applied without tending to change shape. A wheel has a certain amount of thickness, and the file or cutter must pass through it exactly parallel to its axis so that the profile of the tooth as viewed from each side of the wheel is identical. English wheels are made from hardened brass, unlike many wheels on the Continent which are prepared from brass castings. Cast brass is not as hard as brass which has been work-hardened and there is always the danger of blow holes having been formed, but naturally a wheel formed from a casting with the 'crossings' or spokes already prepared, takes a lot less time to finish.

When a toothed wheel has to be made by hand, a lot of careful measurement has to be made to set out the right number of teeth and then the operations with the file have to be carefully and accurately carried out. The final stage is the rounding up, whereby the rectangular shaped tooth is cut to the shape of a Gothic arch to allow it to engage and disengage neatly with the pinion. To file such a wheel requires a steady hand, an accurate eye and all the patience in the world. A mistake near the end of the job means a lot of wasted work and starting all over again.

THE WHEEL-CUTTING ENGINE

Large-scale production of clocks and watches could never have taken place without some mechanical means of cutting wheels. The invention of the wheel-cutting engine is usually ascribed to Robert Hooke and the earliest machines of this nature could have been produced during the time that he was associated with Tompion. When one examines such clocks as those by Jost Burgi, now in the museum at Kassel, which were produced about 1600, one cannot help feeling that some mechanical form of wheel cutter must have existed at this period. Large wheels containing hundreds of small accurately-cut teeth are found in these clocks and it seems impossible that they could have been produced by the method illustrated by Stradanus.

The basic idea of the wheel-cutting engine is the use of the division plate. For clock engines this is a brass disc about 18 in. in diameter and up to $\frac{1}{4}$ in. thick. A number of concentric circles are engraved on it, the distance between each being about $\frac{1}{4}$ inch. On each circle is drilled a number of holes equally spaced from each other and occupying the entire circle. The numbers chosen are those most commonly used in clockwork such as 96, 72, 60 etc. Lesser numbers can be allowed for by using every third or fourth hole as required. The holes are not drilled right through the plate but are sunk sufficiently deep to allow a stop piece to enter and hold the plate quite firmly while a tooth is being cut. The division plate is rigidly mounted on a vertical spindle supported on a stout frame. The spindle is threaded at its upper end and the wheel blank to be cut is placed on this threaded part and firmly held by a nut. An adjustable frame carries a small train of gears for rotating a cutter, which is a circular file made to a specified size.

The cutter frame can be moved nearer to or further away from the centre as desired and it moves up and down sufficiently to allow the cutter to pass right through the blank being cut. While a cut is being made, the blank is held rigid by the stop piece resting in one of the holes of the division plate and, as soon as the cut has been completed, the division plate is moved one space and the next cut taken while the plate is again held rigid by the stop piece. Today cutters can be made with teeth so shaped that the rounded edges can be made on the wheel-teeth at the same time as the spaces between the teeth are cut, but formerly the cutter just produced a series of rectangular slots, leaving the teeth in a castellated pattern, and they were rounded up by hand afterwards. The tool used was known as a rounding-up

Right Wheel-cutting engine, 18th century, *and above* Wheel-cutting engine showing the cutter and the circles of depressions on the division plate

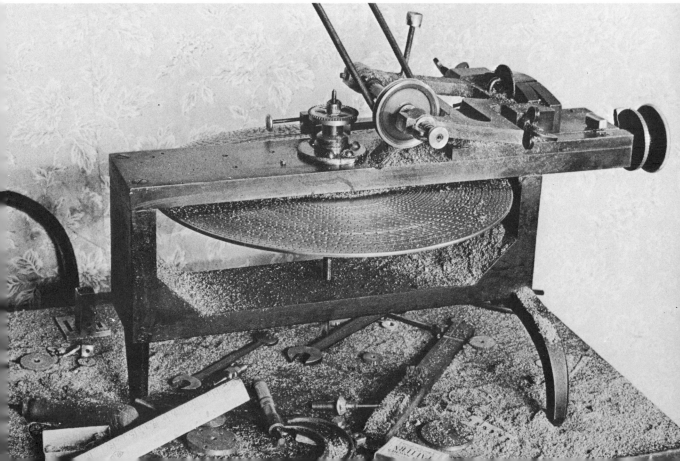

file and in section was like a segment of a circle. Teeth were cut on the flat side only so that the back of the file did not spoil adjacent teeth while the rounding-up was proceeding and the shape of the file allowed it to turn one way or the other without jamming in the available space. Anchor scapewheels had special cutters which had a curved edge on one side and a straight edge on the other.

The cutters were formed by shaping a steel disc to the required outline, cutting teeth on it by hand and then hardening and tempering it. Sometimes a fly cutter was used which was shaped from a piece of steel and in effect consisted of one cutting tooth only. A fly cutter had to rotate at a very high speed but could perform satisfactory work.

The chief precautions to be taken in connection with a wheel-cutting engine are to ensure that the blank is fixed on tightly enough to maintain its relationship with the division plate in spite of all the vibration produced during cutting, and that the blank is supported sufficiently near its edge to provide a firm resistance to the cutter, but not impede it on its passage through the blank. The noise produced is most unpleasant and the work can be very tiring if the cutter is driven by a hand-operated crank. The blank is left solid during cutting to give the maximum rigidity, but afterwards portions of metal are removed from the centre to leave spokes or 'crossings', the process being known as 'crossing out'. Special crossing out files are used for finishing the holes which may be cut by a piercing saw or punched out by a die if a press is available. There may be three or four crossings to the wheel and the inside edges after filing are smoothed and polished. Naturally all burrs from the cutting of the teeth are also removed and the surface of the wheel polished. The extra cleaning and finish of the parts of a clock or watch are not only to give a pleasing appearance to the movement, but also have a practical application as a smooth surface does not attract dirt so much as a rough one. The purpose of crossing out is to make the wheels lighter, thereby saving on the motive power required and so prolong the life of the clock by minimising wear.

MAKING THE ARBORS

The arbors or axles on which the wheels are mounted include the pinions with which the wheels mesh. The arbors are of steel and the wheels are of brass. The teeth of a pinion are generally known as 'leaves' and in theory are supposed to number fewer than twenty. The arbors and pinions were originally filed and turned from a solid piece of steel, but at some period in the seventeenth century pinion wire was invented. This is a steel rod which is drawn through a series of holes in a hardened steel plate which get successively nearer to the outline of the pinion. By the time the last draw has been made, the rod has taken on the profile of the complete pinion. Each arbor is made by cutting a piece of pinion wire a shade longer than the distance between the outer edges of the plates. The ends are filed conically so that they can be carried in the turns and a suitable ferrule is mounted on the rod. The place for the actual pinion is marked by rotating the rod in the turns, with the point of a graver just touching the leaves at the appropriate places, being careful to leave enough to act as a seating for the wheel as well, if it is an arbor where the wheel and

Pinion wire in the rough

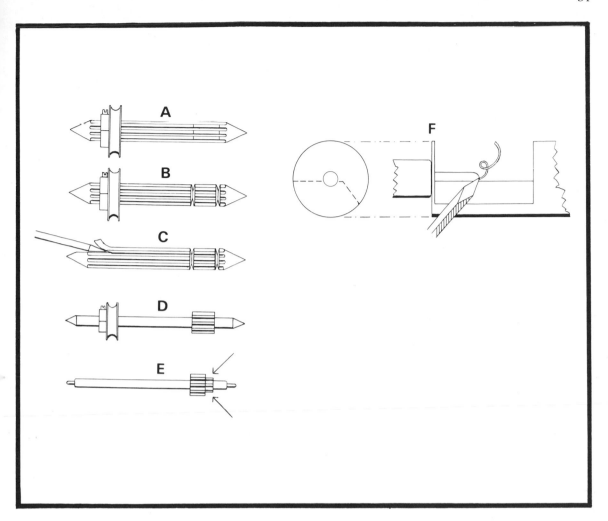

Making a Pinion

[A] shows a piece of pinion wire with the ends pointed for mounting in a turns and a ferrule attached for the bowstring. The position of the pinion has been marked with the point of the graver

[B] The leaves have been cut at the places marked down to the solid part of the arbor

[C] the unwanted portions of the leaves are removed with a chisel-shaped punch

[D] a ferrule has been fitted as the work is now thinner, the edges are cut vertically and the arbor is smoothed and polished

[E] the finished pinion with pivots formed on the ends and leaves cut to make a seating for the wheel (arrowed)

[F] the ends of the pivots being formed on a special hollow runner. The thin circular end with the hole stops endwise movement of the arbor and the groove forms a bed to give the pivot support and prevent it breaking

pinion are together. This arrangement is usually used in the going train with all the wheels near the back plate, so that the power passes to the scapewheel arbor more or less in a straight line. If this were not so, there would be a twisting effect on the arbors causing them to wear their holes more quickly. In the striking train, the design calls for wheels to be at the front or back ends of the arbors alternately, but with the fast running of the striking train, the lubrication is better distributed and the trouble is less apparent.

After the place for the actual pinion leaves has been marked, all the redundant leaves must be cut away on the rest of the arbor. The clockmaker checks his markings and when he is satisfied he replaces the pinion wire in the turns and cuts deeper until the solid centre of the arbor is reached. The arbor is removed from the turns once more and the redundant leaves are then cut away with a chisel, the deep cuts made in the turns preventing the part that is to remain from being removed or damaged. The chisel cut comes from the ends of the arbor towards the part that is being retained. When all the waste leaves have been cut away, a new ferrule is put on the arbor, to allow for the smaller diameter, and the arbor is smoothed and the pivots formed. The operative leaves then have to be reduced to the correct size with a file and then have their faces smoothed. The pinion is then hardened and tempered and the wheel riveted in place, a sharp punch being used to drive the softer brass between the hard leaves of the pinion. Care must be taken that the wheel is absolutely concentric after mounting. After hardening and tempering, the arbor and the leaves are polished.

Some arbors are left extra long. The scape wheel arbor may carry a seconds hand, the centre arbor carries the cannon pinion which supports the minute hand and the third arbor of the striking train carries the gathering pallet, which makes one revolution for each blow struck and in doing so gathers up one tooth at a time of the rack. The rack drops a certain distance at each hour which is determined by a spiral plate called a 'snail', which rotates with the hour hand and the further the rack is allowed to fall, the greater number of blows are sounded. The scape and centre arbors carry what are virtually extended pivots, but the gathering pallet arbor is squared and sometimes drilled with a small hole near its end so that the gathering pallet can be held in position by a tapered pin. Alternatively the end can be threaded and the gathering pallet held in place by a small nut. Some clocks merely have the square tapered and the gathering pallet held by a push-on fit. If the gathering pallet comes loose, it will not gather up the rack, and the clock goes on striking until it runs down. Keeping it in position is one of those tiny details that matter a great deal.

THE DEPTH TOOL

A depth tool is virtually two sets of turns joined at the bottom by a hinge, so that the centre lines of each can be advanced towards or retarded from each other. The runners that fit the tool, have female centres of various sizes to allow for the various sizes of pivots, with extra large ones to take the pivots of a fusee or the barrel of a long case clock. The ends of the runners that do not carry the pivots are finished in sharp points. The tool is used by mounting suitable runners to take the pivots of two arbors which run adjacent to each other, the wheel of one meshing with the pinion of the other. The tool is so set that the sharp points of the runners on one side are level. A screw allows the two halves of the tool to be adjusted until the 'depth', i.e. the distance between the centre lines of the arbors allows the freest running of the wheel and pinion in mesh. When this has been accomplished, the sharp ends of the runners are used as dividers to mark the plate with the positions to drill the holes. If the depth tool is accurately made, the arbors should run smoothly when the plates are assembled, but things do occasionally go astray, and one sometimes sees a plate where a bush has been inserted with signs that the hole was not drilled correctly at the first attempt. A depth tool is useless unless accurately made and not every eighteenth century maker had one.

Having set out the trains, the clockmaker then rivets the two plates together and drills through both where all the holes come, not forgetting the holes for the pillars. When the pillars are later fastened in position, he can then be certain that all the holes are 'upright' i.e. directly opposite each other. Holes are drilled smaller than required and opened out by means of a 'broach', i.e. a tapered steel rod with about six flat surfaces ground on it that cut the circumference of the hole equally. When almost to size, a smooth broach is used which removes very little metal but burnishes and hardens the surface that is to bear the pivots. Brass cannot be hardened by a heating process such as steel can. It can only be

A depth tool in use

hardened by being hammered or being other-wise put under compression. If hardened brass is heated it becomes soft again.

MAKING DRILLS AND THEIR USE

The clockmaker makes his own drills by taking a piece of steel of the appropriate size, hammering one end to spread it, taking care not to hammer it too much, and then filing the end of the flattened part to a point with an angle of about 90°. If the drill is intended for steel, this angle will be greater than if the drill is intended for brass. Formerly drills were mostly used with a to-and-fro motion and each side of the point would be sharpened on both sides giving a scraping action, but when continuous rotation became available, each side was sharpened on the back only and a better cutting action resulted.

When the drill has been made it is hardened by heating it to redness in a small flame and rapidly withdrawing it and waving it in the air. The amount of heat held in the metal is not always sufficient to allow the cooling by oil or water to take place. This process of air cooling is known as 'flirting'. Tempering is done on a brass plate which is gently warmed while the drill is carefully watched for colour, as the changes take place extremely rapidly if too much heat is applied to a small piece of steel. When the drill is of the correct hardness, the edges are sharpened on an oilstone and it is ready for use. Very small drills do not contain enough metal to allow for tempering, and the flirting process has to suffice.

The to-and-fro motion is applied to drills by means of a bow as when using a turns. The drill is put in a holder consisting of a steel rod which has been bored out to take the end of the drill and on which is mounted a brass pulley to take the bowstring. The rear end of the rod is hardened and tempered, and ends in a point which is intended to rest in a hollow in the edge of the vice when the drill is being used. The drill is maintained as far as possible in a horizontal position. The piece being drilled is held against the drill point after a punch mark

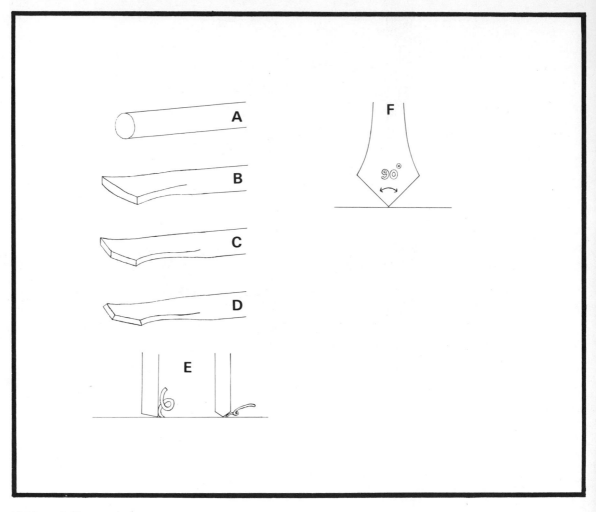

Making a Drill

[A] a rod of steel with smaller diameter than the blade of the drill

[B] the end of the rod is flattened to form the blade

[C] the blade is filed to a point

[D] the ends are chamfered to give a cutting edge

[E] *left* the cutting action for continuous motion, *right* the cutting action for to-and-fro motion

[F] the angle of the edges of a drill for brass, a steel drill needs a much wider angle

has been made at the place where the hole is to be drilled to allow the drill to get a start. The end of the drill is secured in the holder by a screw. An easier method to hold it without cutting a thread, is to cut the back end of the drill to a chamfer with a sharp point. A cut is then made in the side of the holder near the end of the bore until the latter is exposed, and then the chamfer is allowed to project into this cut portion. The drill is then forced to rotate with the holder.

The drill is kept horizontal by mounting a loose ring on the holder. Any tendency for the drill to rise or fall while it is rotating would be indicated by the ring travelling to one side or the other; while the drill remains horizontal the ring will stay in the same place. Frequent sharpening of the drills is necessary especially when cutting steel, as a blunt drill rubs on the bottom of the hole and burnishes it, making a very hard surface which is difficult to remove.

It is important that the cutting edge is the widest part of the drill, otherwise the shank would bind in the hole. This is the reason for spreading the end when the drill is made, and in addition, the flattening of the drill caused by the spreading allows the swarf to escape as it is cut. Drills have to be frequently removed to clear the holes, as the swarf tends to accumulate behind the cut and can cause sufficient interference to break the drill. Steel needs a lubricant such as turpentine, while brass is usually cut dry. If excessive heat builds

Drilling with a Bow Drill

The work is held against the point of the drill. A ring is hung on the drill shank to show whether the drill is remaining horizontal. The ferrule is turned by the bowstring and the pivot rests in a special indentation made on the left side of the vice

Below shows how the drill is forced to move by its tapered rear end projecting through the hole in the ferrule

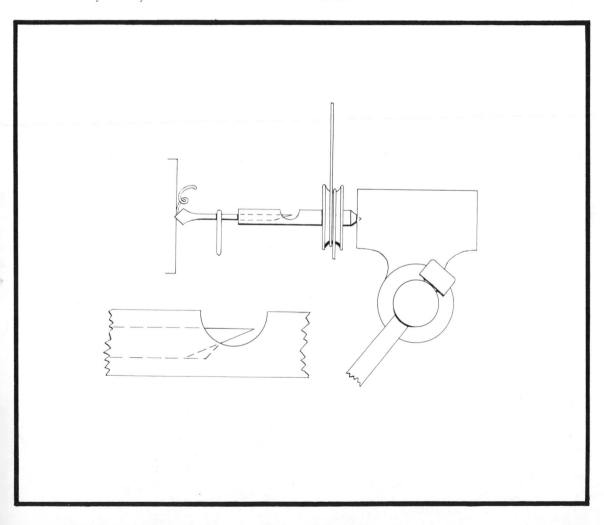

36

up, the temper of the drill is lost and consequently the edge becomes blunt and tends to burnish the work.

ASSEMBLING THE FRAME

After the holes have been drilled, the riveting is broken and the plates are separated again. The pillars are probably made from pieces of brass rod which may have been cast, but as they do not undergo mechanical wear this is not of great importance. The pillars are finished by turning, and then smoothed and polished. The holes in the back plates to receive them, are chamfered on their outer sides and then the pillars are riveted in, a large number of light blows being used which force the metal well into the holes and ensure a good rigid fit. The rigidity of the frame is one of the outstanding features of an old English clock. The front plate is slipped into position over

the ends of the pillars and the pillar ends marked where the top edge comes so that they can be drilled to receive the taper pins that hold the front plate firmly on. The pin wheel and the warning wheel on the striking train have to have their rims drilled to take pins, in one case to raise the hammer and in the other to hold the striking train after 'warning' just before the hour. The pins are riveted in position and any roughness made during the riveting is smoothed away.

STRIKE MECHANISMS

Behind the dial of the clock is the mechanism which releases and locks the striking train together with the motion work which allows the hands to rotate at the 1:12 ratio, and the date mechanism if any. The latter was more important in the days before calendars were given away or easily purchased and the phase

English Long-Case movements. *Left* a 30-hour movement with strike controlled by a count wheel. *Right* an 8-day movement with rack and snail striking mechanism. The wheel below meshes with a wheel of half its size carried round with the hour hand and rotates once in 24 hours so shifting the calendar mechanism

of the moon indicator was also important before street lighting became general. People only went out at night if the moon were bright. These latter mechanisms are worked by a pin that went round with the hour hand and are consequently moved one tooth every twelve hours. More rarely a 2:1 gearing was taken from the hour hand pipe so that a wheel could be driven making one revolution in twenty four hours, and this carried the pin for actuating the date or moonphase mechanism. The striking is locked by levers or 'lifting pieces' which are carried on brass tubes riding on steel studs screwed on to the front plate. The ends of the studs are drilled to take taper pins to prevent the pieces from working off the stud. The lifting pieces are made from steel forgings and are finished with a file and then smoothed. The brass tubes would be made from brass rod roughly shaped in the turns and then drilled as near the centre as possible. Once this hole had been made, the piece could be mounted on a turning arbor, replaced in the turns and finished. The centre of the turning arbor would determine the centre line of the piece and after it was finished the hole would be concentric.

THE PALLETS

The pallets are prepared from a forging. The scapewheel arbor is pushed through a piece of paper until the wheel itself rests on the paper and then the shape of the pallets is drawn on the paper and the forging filed until it nearly corresponds with the drawing. When it is almost right, it is temporarily mounted on its arbor and the wheel and pallets are tried in the depth tool. When finally correct, the pallets are hardened, tempered and mounted permanently on the arbor, usually by means of a brass collet and soft solder. Those wheels in the train that are not mounted directly on to their pinions are usually fastened to their arbors by this method. The acting faces of the pallets are polished. The pallet arbor is supported at the rear by a brass bridge which is fastened to the back plate by two screws and carries a slotted extension for holding the pendulum suspension spring. This bridge and the bridge that carries the hour wheel on the

front plate, are formed from a casting. The various castings were sometimes made by the clockmakers themselves or alternatively procured from a brassfounder, possibly being made from the clockmaker's own wooden patterns.

WORKING WITHOUT A DESIGN BOOK

As our clockmaker is working from a design book, we ought to consider the man who has not inherited this information and is designing his own movements. He will have worked on plenty of movements during his apprenticeship, and may have made notes of the layout of the trains and the numbers of teeth in the wheels, but when it comes to making a movement of his own design he will have to determine the dimensions and arrangement of the various parts, albeit that the layout of the movement will be on very conventional lines. After he has made a rough sketch of the general arrangement, the chief problem he has to solve is the actual size of the parts. Wheel sizes can be selected as he pleases, but once the sizes and numbers of teeth in the wheels have been determined, he has to be very careful to select the right sizes of pinions to gear with them. He can put the pinion sizes on his drawing and hope that he gets them right, but if the size is incorrect he may waste a lot of work and have to replace the pinions that he makes. When working with pinion wire it is possible to make the thickness and diameter of the leaves to an infinite number of sizes, so it is best not to gamble but use a tool designed to compare wheels and pinions accurately, which is known as a 'sector'.

THE SECTOR AND ITS USE

The sector consists of two strips of brass joined by a pivot in such a way that the inner edges of the strips pass through the centre of the pivot. This is accomplished by making small extension pieces at the place where the pivot is to come. Furthermore, the edges must be absolutely straight. An arc is fitted to one arm of the sector and the other arm rides over it. Provision is made for fastening the strips

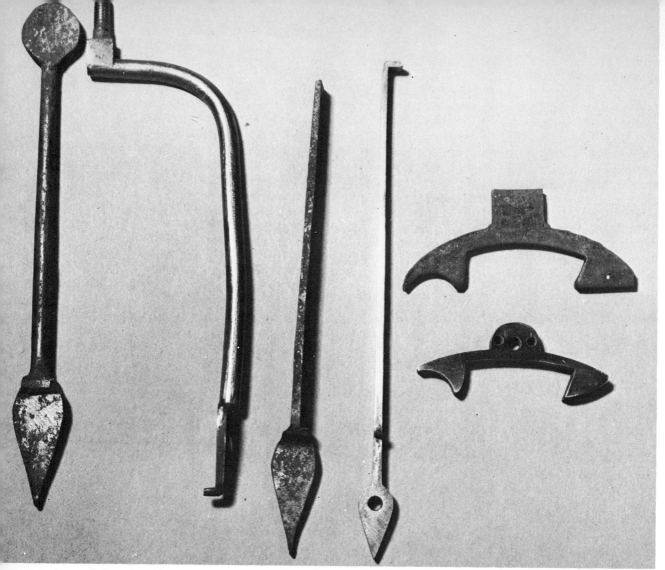

Bell support, hammer springs and pallets; rough forgings and finished, *and below* a sector

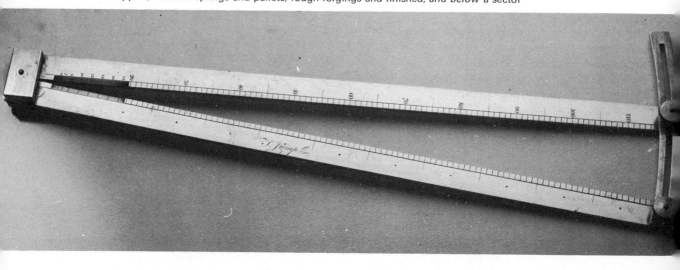

so that they can be held at any angle by means of a wing nut on the arc. Lines are engraved on the arc to show the extent of opening. The two inner edges of the sector are accurately divided into 120 parts, the zero mark coming on the centre of the pivot and the 120 mark near the outer end of the strip. The arc is so engraved that when the sector is opened so that the '100' marks are exactly 1 inch apart, the edge of the arm that slides over the arc is co-incident with the line marked '1 inch'. When the 100 marks are $\frac{1}{2}$ inch apart, the arc reading is '$\frac{1}{2}$ inch' and so on. Between '0' and '20' the edges of the strips are chamfered away to help in sizing pinions and the divisions are displaced from their theoretical position. The 6 mark is not at 6/20 of the distance between 0 and 20 but 1/30 higher, the 7 mark is not midway between 6 and 8 but 1/20 of the distance between 6 and 8 nearer to 6. 6 to 8 is 2/20 of the whole distance from 0 to 20, and 8 to 10, 10 to 12, 14 to 16 and 16 to 18 the same. 18 to 20 is, of course, much smaller than its theoretical size.

In practice, most pinions have between 6 and 12 leaves, and it has been found that it is better to make them a little larger than their theoretical size as would be determined by a sector divided equally, hence the disturbance of the regular spacing. To size wheels and pinions, the wheel is put between the limbs of the sector at the point indicated by the number of its teeth. The correct size of the pinion is then measured by the distance between the limbs at a point indicated by the number of leaves that the pinion is desired to have.

The sector can also be used to determine the sizes for wheels and pinions when preparing a design, but in this case should be divided equally throughout. The calculations are based on the 'pitch circles', i.e. the diameters of the wheel and pinion if their edges touched each other without having teeth. In practice, wheels and pinions are larger than their pitch circles as the teeth and leaves engage each other. This length of tooth or leaf beyond the pitch circle is called the 'addendum'. If it is desired to have a wheel of 60 teeth engaging with a pinion of 8 leaves, their centres being 0·75 inches apart, the numbers of the teeth and

leaves are added, making 68 and the sector is opened until the distance at 68 on the scale is equal to 1$\frac{1}{2}$ inches, i.e. twice the distance between the centres. The width between the centres at 60 now represents the pitch diameter of the wheel and that at 8 that of the pinion. The full diameters are obtained from tables which in the days we are considering would have been compiled by trial and error. The scientific study of gearing only began in the eighteenth century. The sector can also be used as a measuring tool. If the limbs are set so that the 100 marks are one inch apart, the distance at 90 is 0·9 inches and so on.

BARRELS AND LINES

Our clock movement is now almost complete except for the barrels. These are castings which are turned to the appropriate diameter and which then have a spiral groove cut on them. Some makers omitted the spiral groove and left the surfaces plain, but the majority were in favour of the groove. The ends of the barrel are made of sheet brass and are brazed on, the barrel being firmly fixed to its arbor, which is made from a thick rod of steel. In the cover is a large hole which allows access to the line, which is inserted in a hole in the barrel body and then threaded out through the hole in the cover when a knot can be tied. The end is touched with a flame or a piece of hot iron, causing it to sear and prevent the knot coming untied. The knot is then pushed inside the barrel through the large hole.

The lines for an eight-day clock are made from catgut, which in spite of its name is made from the intestines of a sheep. The mucous membrane and fatty matter are removed by scraping after a prolonged soaking in frequently changed water. The intestines are then soaked in fresh water for a night after which they receive a soaking in a potash mixture. They are then passed through an open brass thimble several times which smooths and equalises them. Treatment in a vessel containing the fumes of burning sulphur ensures that any fleshy matter still adhering is destroyed, which would otherwise lead to putrefaction. Lines for clocks must be thin, strong and

A fusee engine, watch size. As the fusee rotates, the tool point is automatically moved along it

durable and are made from small intestines slit up lengthwise by a couple of razor blades fitted into a ball of wood which serves as a guide. The wet gut being drawn over the ball is divided and guided by the operator into the basin beneath. This operation is one of considerable delicacy and when performed well the gut is divided into strips of perfect regularity with great rapidity. A number of these strips are twisted together and given the sulphur treatment.

The weights of an eight-day clock are 'compounded', i.e. they do not hang from the ends of the lines but from pulleys supported in a loop of the line, one end of the latter being passed through the seat board and tied round a small peg which prevents its being pulled through. In this way, the fall of the weight can be limited to about five feet, although twice as much line will have come off the barrel, and the weights have to be rather more than twice as heavy as weights fastened to the end of the line direct, in order to overcome the extra friction. The pulley is made by mounting a brass disc on a turning arbor and turning it in the throw or turns. The pulley runs on a steel bearing supported between two brass bosses which are connected below by a loop of brass or iron, which in its turn supports the hook for the weight. When fastening the gut line, the clockmaker has to know exactly how

high the seat board will be above the floor in the finished case, so it can be arranged for the weight still to be hanging after all the line has come off the barrel. If the weight touches the floor, the line will go slack, and the twist in it will cause it to coil up and become tangled, with the possibility of chafing and subsequent breakage when the clock is wound. A line too long also causes the barrel grooves to be filled with line before the weight is at its maximum height and further winding lays line over the top of that already in the groove. The final adjustments to the length of the line are made by winding any slack round the small peg which prevents it from being pulled through the seat board. The lines have to be kept supple by the application of some animal oil, or else they would dry out and break with the possibility of damage being caused by the falling weight.

THE PENDULUM

The construction of the pendulum calls for little comment. The bob is made from spun brass discs covering a piece of lead which is pierced by a hole of rectangular section allowing the bob to slide onto the rectangular piece of brass which carries it. This piece of brass has a piece of threaded rod at the bottom which receives the rating nut which supports the bob and allows the clock to be regulated. The suspension spring is firmly gripped by the brass jaws on the bridge supporting the rear pallet arbor and is riveted to the impulse block which works in the rectangular loop of the crutch and provides the connection between pendulum and escapement. Even as early as the beginning of the eighteenth century it is highly probable that our clockmaker will obtain his dial and hands from a specialist craftsman. The spandrels at the corner of the dial will be castings obtained from London which will probably be reproduced locally later to the detriment of the sharpness of the design.

SPRING-DRIVEN STRIKING CLOCKS

If our clockmaker were constructing a spring-driven striking clock, the work undertaken would be basically the same except that the anchor escapement would be replaced by a verge escapement and short pendulum, and the weight-drive through grooved barrels would be replaced by springs in plain barrels driving the clock through gut lines operating on fusees. The plain barrels would be built up of sheet brass bent round a former and soldered. The bottom of the barrel consists of a disc of brass let into a groove cut on the edge of the barrel and soldered into position, while the cover is a similar disc at the other end of the barrel but is held by a snap in fit and is removable. The grooves in the barrel edges would be somewhat difficult to cut using a turns, on account of their large diameter of 2 to 3 inches, so the best way to make them would be to mount the barrel on a cylindrical piece of wood with a hole through the centre and mount this on an arbor in the throw. The covers would be finished in the throw, mounted on turning arbors. The cover is thickened in the centre to form a bearing surface, for the barrel rotates on its arbor as the clock goes while the arbor itself remains stationary and the thick portion also helps to strengthen the cover and take a bearing on the shoulders of the arbor preventing too much 'endshake'. Endshake is play in a direction parallel to the centre line of the arbor. The barrel arbors are turned from substantial pieces of forged steel and the hook for holding the inner end of the mainspring is screwed into the arbor and then shaped.

CUTTING FUSEES

The fusees have to be cut on a special fusee-cutting engine and probably not many clock-makers possessed these tools. They are expensive and it consumes a lot of time to make one's own, so the obvious solution is to get the fusees cut by a specialist workshop. It has been suggested previously that specialist facilities were begun by Tompion, and the only limit to the development of this idea would have been the availability of transport. In theory, every mainspring needs its own specially cut fusee and if the spring of a clock is changed, the fusee should be tested and amended as well, but with pendulum control the fusee is of lesser importance, and with an anchor or dead beat escapement a clock shows less variation than with a verge escapement. There would not be much temptation to amend a fusee that had been obtained from a specialist workshop. Our clockmaker would therefore have finished the fusee arbors and mounted the fusees on the great wheels after having provided the necessary clickwork.

Fusees are tested by means of an appliance

The Testing Rod. The jaws at the left side are adjustable to fit the winding square on the fusee. The spherical weight can be moved to any position and secured by the thumbscrew

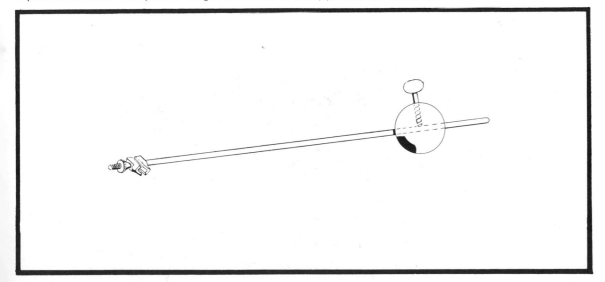

which consists of a long rod provided with adjustable jaws which can be fitted on to the winding square of the fusee. On the rod is a movable weight which can be fixed in any position. The fusee and barrel are placed between the plates, and the spring wound by placing the square loop on the winding square and using the rod as a lever. After the spring has been wound, it is allowed to run down under control, the shifting weight on the rod being moved away from the square until there is just enough power to rotate it. Any points where it accelerates, indicate that the fusee diameter is too large at that point and vice versa. If it is too large, the groove can be deepened at that point, but if it is too small, the only remedy is to recut the fusee with subsequent adjustment as necessary.

CUTTING SCREWS

Screws were not used in clockwork until the mid sixteenth century, but by the eighteenth were well established. Screw cutters made on similar principles to fusee engines were known, but the commonest method of screw-cutting was by means of dies or a screwplate. A screwplate consists of a steel plate containing a number of holes of graduated size, each hole carrying a thread which has been cut in it by means of a tap. After the plate has been made it is hardened, but only slightly tempered in order to leave the steel as hard as possible. If a rod of metal is held tightly in a vice and a suitably sized hole in the screwplate placed on it and the plate rotated under pressure, the thread of the screwplate is forced on to the metal rod. The action is somewhat different from the cutting action of modern screw-plates and needs a lot of force and a steady hand, care being taken not to break the piece being worked on. The taps for making the screwplate are made from steel, and the thread is cut by means of a chaser. This is a tool with several points on its side at the same distance apart as the threads which it is desired to cut. The tap is rotated slowly in the throw and the chaser forced along it, the leading point cutting the thread and the following points deepening it. The travel of the chaser must remain constant in relation to the speed of rotation if an even thread is to be made. The taps are hardened and tempered after making. After taps have been used for cutting a screwplate they can be kept for threading holes in parts that are to be made.

Screws in early clocks have square heads. This enables them to be held in the vice while the shank is being cut by means of the screw-plate. Round-headed screws are more difficult to grip and would only have been made when necessary for appearance. Under modern manufacturing methods round-headed screws can be easily produced.

Screwplates and taps

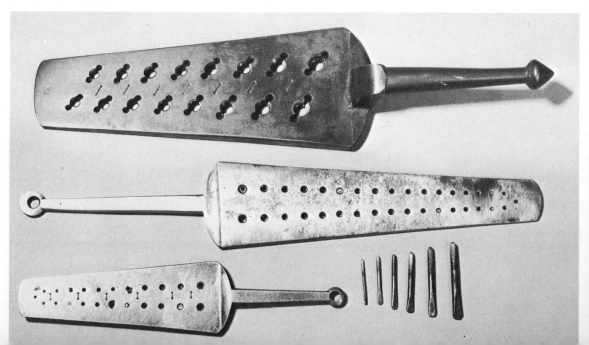

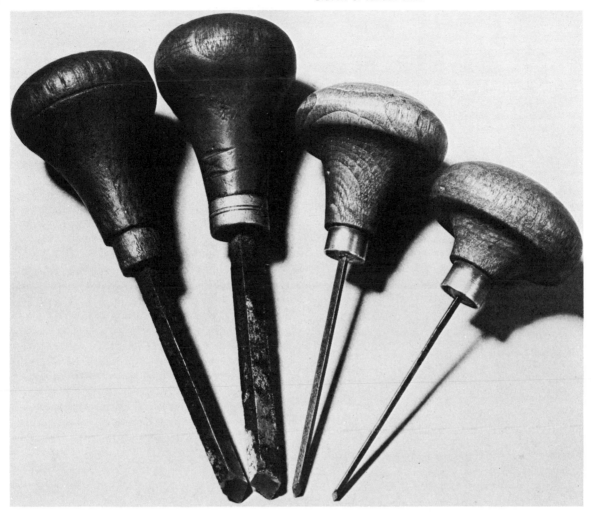

4 TOOLS AND TECHNIQUES OF THE EARLY CLOCKMAKERS

Turning is so important to a watch or clockmaker that it is necessary to go into some detail in order to describe the various processes involved. The basic apparatus, whether a turns or throw is being used, consists of a base bar supporting one fixed head and one movable one. The latter slides along the bar, which must be perfectly straight and smooth, and can be fixed at any desired point, allowing for pieces of work of any length within the range of travel of the loose head. The heads themselves are bored with circular holes parallel to the bed which carry the runners which actually support the work. The runners can be held with more or less of their length protruding

Turns Runners

[A] plain points where female centres are formed on work

[B] Female centres in runners; work is pointed. In A and B note clearance for points at bottom of centre

[C] Similar to B but part of runner is cut away to allow tool to approach work more closely

[D] Work supported off centre for accommodating pivot in adjustable bed

[E] Polisher for pivot maintained at correct height by adjustable screw

[F], [G] Runner for finishing conical end of work before inserting in turns. The pressure of the triangular stone keeps the work from advancing to the right

[H] Making an adjustable pivot bed. The outer circle represents the diameter of the runner. The arrow indicates the distance that the opposite runner is offset

[I] Six holes drilled on the inner circle

[J] Runner is cut away to inner circle leaving semicircular beds

and are fastened by a thumbscrew. It is important that the holes are exactly in line so that the work runs exactly parallel to the bed. Where the work is carried in hollow runners, it must not bind in the sides of the holes as this entails extra friction and makes for inaccurate working. The work is supported at each end with the minimum amount of support possible to save friction and leave the maximum amount of metal free to be operated on. The work is driven by a ferrule which occupies some of the area of the piece, and if this portion has to be worked on, the ferrule must be removed and placed elsewhere. Another ferrule is required if it has to fit on a part of another diameter. In the throw, it is possible to drive the work by a carrier, but this also

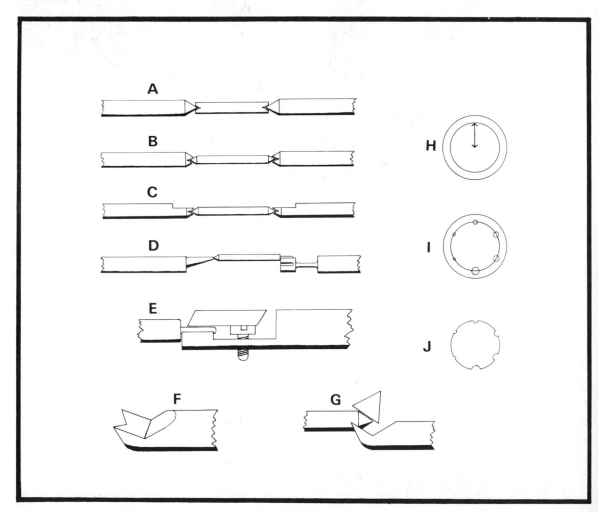

The ferrules with the threads are for mounting wheels in the turns. The arbors with the tapered shanks are for turning hollow pieces such as bushes

occupies some part of the working surface and may have to be moved if necessary. One big advantage of work turned between dead centres is that it can be removed from the turns or throw and be replaced and still be true, which is not the case with a lathe using collets or chucks.

THE RUNNERS

The runners are made of steel rod which exactly fit the holes which receive them and are capable of being fixed in any position. For maximum rigidity, the heads are kept as close together as possible with the runners projecting the minimum amount to avoid too much overhang. A large number of runners are useful, each type being made in several different sizes to accommodate different types of work. The old clock and watch-makers made their own and built up a large collection over years

of work. Sometimes special runners would be made for a certain job and then held in stock and perhaps not used again for a long time. The simplest runners merely have their ends turned to a cone forming a male centre. When these are used, the work has to be drilled at each end, allowing sufficient clearance for the points. The next simplest type is made in the same way, but the points are turned off and a small conical hole is made in the end of the runner. This means that the work needs to bear sharp points at its ends which are usually produced by a file whilst rotating the work on the edge of a block of wood with the fingers or with the aid of a pinvice. The angle of the points should be the same as that of the sides of the small conical hole in the runner in order to give the correct bearing surface.

A variation of this type of runner is made where the conical end is filed away flat for almost half the thickness of the runner to the

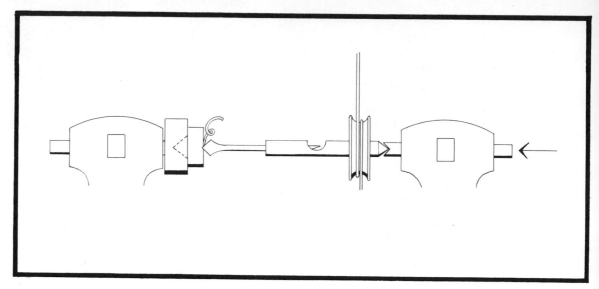

Drilling in the Turns.
The work is held against a flat-headed runner. The dotted lines indicate a clearance hole for the drill to enter as it passes through the work. The runner supporting the end of the ferrule is advanced in the direction arrowed

very edge of the conical depression. This allows the turning tool to approach much closer to the end of the piece being dealt with and is therefore used for pivot turning. When a pivot has been formed with the aid of this type of runner, the end is rounded by supporting it in a hollow runner which has had almost all the metal filed away near its end and only a thin ring left to support the pivot. The shoulder of the pivot bears against the runner and the tool can be rested on the cut away portion.

Jacot tool for polishing pivots

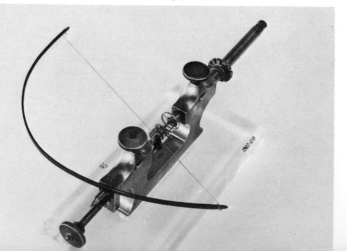

POLISHING PIVOTS

Polishing of pivots is done by a pair of special runners. One is filed to a point off-centre with a small depression in it and the other bears a head with a radius slightly larger than the distance the other is off-centre. The actual offset is marked on the end of the large head and a circle made using this distance as radius. Six or so holes of increasing size are drilled equidistantly on this circle and the head is then turned away to the circle, leaving semi-circular channels or beds on the surface. If one end of an arbor is then supported in the first off-centre runner, and the bed appropriate to the size of the pivot is brought round to support the other, a polisher can be applied. This holds the work down while the rotation of the arbor with the bow causes a polished surface to form on the pivot. Specially designed turns for this purpose are sold under the name 'Jacot Tool' but the ordinary turns is quite useful for polishing pivots. Another form of polishing runner has a bed in its end on the centre line, just behind this the runner is filed somewhat thinner and a screw is inserted on the flat portion. The polisher is supported partly by the pivot being worked on and partly by the screw which can be screwed in or out until the top of its head is exactly level with the top surface of the

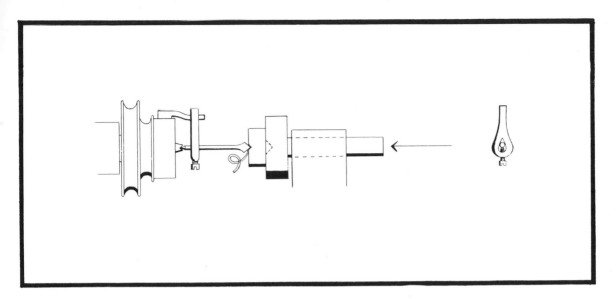

pivot. This guides the polisher to polish the pivot equally all along.

TURNING ARBORS AND FERRULES

Drilling in the Throw.
The drill is supported by a female centre in the headstock and driven by the projecting finger through a carrier. The work is held against a flat-headed runner which is advanced as arrowed as the drill penetrates. The dotted lines indicate a clearance hole for the drill point. The carrier is shown separately on the right

Turning arbors are used for making a wheel collet or reducing a bush in size or in fact for operating on any piece of metal with a hole through its centre. These are pieces of steel which slightly taper throughout their length and have points at each end for placing in runners with female centres. The arbors have a brass pulley near the thicker end for taking the string of the bow. The work is placed on the arbor at the smaller end and pushed further on until the taper makes it grip. It is then possible to rotate the arbor between the centres with the bow and cut the work with a turning tool. Arbors are supplied in sets with a very slight difference between each to allow for a great number of sizes of the central hole in the work, but of course in days gone by, the clockmakers would make their own producing a number of useful sizes to begin with and adding to the series later as special jobs required extra sizes.

The ferrules for use with the turns, are discs of steel with a hole through the centre. The discs are split across the centre and each half carries a lug which allows the two parts to be screwed tightly together. A number of discs of the same size may have slight differences in their centre holes to accommodate different sizes of work, as it is important that the two halves of the disc are screwed tightly together and at the same time have a firm grip on the work. If the two halves were not firmly together, the edges might fray the string of the bow. On the edge of the disc a groove is cut to take the string, and as the discs become smaller in size a smaller bow is substituted with horsehair instead of a gut line or other cord. The bow is generally made of whalebone but sometimes of cane or metal. Some ferrules are solid with a slightly tapered hole in the middle, these can be used on tapered arbors but for parallel ones the split ferrules are more certain. The larger the diameter of the work being turned so should the diameter of the ferrule be larger, a ferrule that is too small does not give enough leverage and the work stops as soon as the tool begins to cut.

THE GRAVER

The tool used for turning by hand is known as a graver, and consists of a bar of steel, of square or lozenge shaped section which is ground off at one corner, leaving a flat face, the edge of which is presented to the work. The tool is sharpened by rubbing the flat face on a stone with a circular movement and just one wipe given on the stone to the sides to remove the feather edge. The tools for turning can nowadays be sharpened on a modern artificially produced stone, but in previous centuries only natural sharpening stones would have been available. Gravers are usually made in various sizes from $\frac{1}{8}$ in. to $\frac{3}{16}$ in. measured on the side, but larger or smaller sizes can be made for special jobs as desired. The correct way of cutting is to present the edge of the tool, just behind the point, to the place where it is desired to cut and moving the tool away from the point. If correctly applied, the tool will remove shavings from the metal and not dust. The correct height is a fraction above the centre and the tool is held on an adjustable toolrest which can be varied in height and secured to the central bar of the turns or throw at any position between the two heads. The usual rest supplied is rather long, and the clockmaker will often make one or two more which are much narrower, as they are better for supporting the tool when the piece being worked upon is small.

The normal graver is square in section, but the lozenge shaped graver is used for making deeper cuts, this latter tool is naturally weaker, and it is easy to break its point if it is not carefully handled. Gravers should be kept sharp and frequently inspected for worn cutting edges. A blunt graver will burnish the work and make it hard to cut.

DRILLING WITH A TURNS

The turns or throw can also be used for drilling. The drill is held in a special drill ferrule with its point supported in a female centre, in a runner which is loose in the head. The point of the drill is pressed against the work in a tiny punch mark which has been made to indicate the spot where the hole is to be drilled. The work is held against a flat-ended runner in the other head of the turns and this runner is fixed by its clamping screw. A hole should be provided to receive the drill point if the work is to be drilled right through. The drill ferrule is rotated by the bow and pressure applied to the drill through the unsecured runner. If the throw is being used, the flat-ended runner can be held in the sliding head and not fixed, while the drill is held at the fixed head and rotated by a carrier. The work is pressed onto the drill by pressure on the flat-ended runner from the end opposite to the work. Both these methods require constant pressure between the drill and the work, for as soon as this pressure is released, the various parts will fall.

RE-PIVOTING AN ARBOR

One of the commonest jobs that has to be done using a turns or throw for drilling, is to re-pivot an arbor. Here the problem is mainly to drill the arbor so that the hole is true, for the slightest eccentricity will affect the depthing between the arbor concerned and those adjacent to it. In turning between dead centres each end of the work has to be supported, so the end to be drilled is held by the conical mouth of a hole in a steel piece that fits into the end of a hollow runner. A set of these pieces is needed, for although the conical openings may be the same or similar in all of them, the central hole will differ, as the drills used will need to be larger or smaller according to the size of the pivot. The drill has to fit this hole very closely in order to be held firmly on the centre line while the initial piercing of the arbor is taking place. The drill is held in a tubular holder which fits closely into the hole of the hollow runner, and the point goes through the hole in the supporting piece and so is able to drill the arbor in the correct place. Frequent withdrawal of the drill is necessary to clear the swarf and ensure that the cutting edges are still sharp. The hole is bored to about the same depth as the pivot should protrude, and then a piece of pivot steel is tapped home and the pivot proper finished on the runners described previously. After a pivot has been formed, it is smoothed by a file which is of trapezium section so that the shoulder is not cut by it, and then burnished. If a pivot breaks on an arbor which has its pinion head adjacent to the end where the pivot is broken, it is often safer to scrap the old arbor and make a new one rather than risk drilling and breaking the pinion.

When a long arbor is being turned between dead centres it may have enough play in the centre to bring the two ends closer together and cause them to leave their supports. For this reason the centre of the arbor is supported by means of a 'steady', i.e. a vertical steel rod with a triangular notch filed in it horizontally, which can be brought to support the work exactly on the centre line and prevent whipping. The steady is hardened and tempered and then polished. It is placed nearer to or further from the centre line according to the diameter of the work, which is supported by the top and bottom of the notch.

There are many small objects such as screws which it is difficult to support at each end in dead-centre turning and a tool was therefore evolved to hold these pieces in a kind of vice or 'chuck'. It was provided with continuous rotation like the throw and was driven by a handwheel at the rear. Tools such as this were the forerunners of the modern watchmaker's lathe. There was a limit to the size of pieces that could be held in the chucks and the selection of the latter was very limited.

After a pivot has been formed, or a part of a clock which is subjected to friction is ready for finishing, it has its surface worked on by a burnisher. A burnisher is best likened to a file without any teeth. The tool can be made in various shapes such as those of the commonest files, and mounted with similar handles. It is used for finishing pivots in the turns or throw in conjunction with the special runners previously mentioned, which have beds for receiving the pivots. The burnisher is trimmed by making very light movements across it with a fine file, and after being slightly moistened, is then applied to the pivot while it is being rotated. As the top edge of the pivot moves towards the operator, the burnisher is pushed forward and vice versa. It has to remain in contact with the rotating piece being worked on in order to keep it in position on

Below left Pivoting. The end of the arbor is supported by the conical mouth of the end piece of the runner, different sizes are available which screw into the runner. The inside diameter of the runner end holds the drill on the centre line and ensures that it enters the centre of the arbor
Right Steady. The position of the steady is adjusted until the slot supports the work and prevents whipping

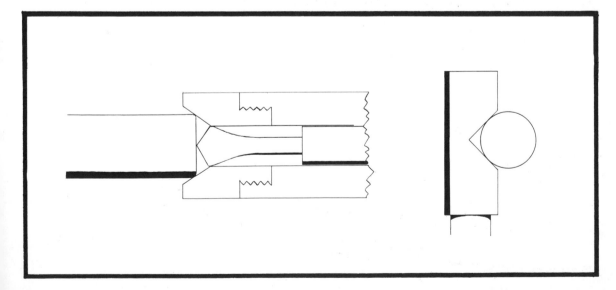

Screw lathe

Screw head tool and collets

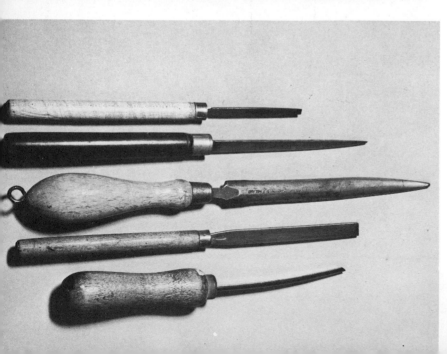

Burnishers

its bed. The burnisher is moistened with saliva, water or other liquid chosen by the watch-maker, and when burnishing is complete, the work bears a mirror-like finish which not only helps the pivot to run with less friction but is also harder than before.

A WATCH-MAKER'S LATHE

Although not strictly in chronological order, it will now be convenient to describe the use of the watch-maker's lathe. Those who have used both a lathe and a turns will have been impressed by the speed and convenience of the former compared to the latter, but the turns is still useful for many jobs that require sensitivity of touch and also possesses the great advantage of allowing the work to be removed and replaced without its running out of true. The lathe allows work to be supported at one end only, and the continuous rotation speeds up the actual cutting, but in some cases the speed of cutting may be a disadvantage as too much metal can be removed and the part spoiled.

The lathe basically consists of a bed which is usually a bar of circular section accurately finished and with a flat formed along one side to allow the 'tailstock' or toolrest to be held firmly without tending to turn. Some beds

have a channel formed in them for the same purpose. The bar is fixed in the 'headstock' which is a firm base carrying the bearings for the spindle, which in a watchmaker's lathe is hollow and should be as rigid as possible and hardened. The operative end carries a conical depression into which the chucks or collets are fitted, and a tube with an internal thread is inserted in the hollow spindle and screwed on to the end of the chuck or collet drawing it into the cone and holding it very firmly. In the case of split chucks, the action closes the jaws on the work being held. Split chucks and other forms of holder for work have a keyway that coincides with a key in the spindle and allows insertion only in one position, as

Right lorch lathe set up for holding work by a collet
Below lorch lathe set up for holding work by a mandrel; the part being operated upon is a watch plate

accessories must always fit accurately. The spindle carries two or three pulleys to which the driving belt is applied. The angle of the grooves in the pulleys should be fairly small to allow the driving belt to get a good grip.

The hollow spindle and split chuck were invented by C. S. Moseley of the Boston Watch Company of U.S.A. and his improved model of 1859 was the forerunner of the modern lathe. Webster of the American Watch Company began to make lathes about this time. In 1879 he formed a partnership with Whitcombe and founded the American Watch Tool Company. His Webster Whitcombe lathe of 1889 set the standard for subsequent tools. Although first produced in America, the watch-maker's lathe was taken up by Continental manufacturers. In the 1880s a watch-maker's lathe cost £8 to £12 while a turns could be had for a few shillings, so it is little wonder that sales were not great although they were on the increase. In 1896 it was estimated that 90% of all watch-makers in Britain were still using turns. The facility of the turns for keeping work true was an important consideration. Continental watch-makers often use the lathe with the headstock on the right, and although this makes no difference to the finished work it seems awkward to the British watchmaker.

The split chuck is the most important method of holding work in the lathe, but there are many other forms of holder intended to deal with work of various shapes and sizes. Step chucks are made on the lines of the split chucks but are of larger diameter, and have a number of concentric steps turned in them for holding wheels or discs. Wax chucks or cement chucks are intended for holding the work by means of shellac or cement, and are generally flat discs with concentric circles on them for helping to locate the work. When work is to be applied to the chuck, the latter is rotated in the lathe and the spirit lamp applied to it to warm the shellac. As soon as this is soft, the work is pressed on to it, and while the chuck is rotating it is centralised and held by a piece of pegwood. When the work is running true, the shellac is allowed to cool. Another variety of wax chuck is made hollow, so the recess can be filled with shellac and only the end of the piece is worked on, e.g. a balance staff is embedded in the shellac while the pivot is receiving attention. When the job is finished, the chuck with the work adhering to it is boiled in a spoon of methylated spirit which dissolves the shellac.

ATTACHMENTS FOR THE LATHE

Self-centring chucks with reversible jaws are also made for use in a watch-maker's lathe and are very useful for the rapid and accurate securing of larger pieces than can be conveniently held in split chucks. A faceplate with adjustable dogs can be used for holding watch plates or other irregularly shaped pieces of metal. A disc with a driving pin is also made to fit into the lathe for turning between centres by means of a carrier, and male and female centres of various sizes can be fitted into it.

The toolrest for lathe turning is very similar to that used on the turns or throw, but the lathe has the advantage that a slide-rest can also be employed. This holds a tool rigidly and allows it to be moved towards or away from the centre of the work and also in a direction parallel to the bed. The tools are ground so that the edge forms the widest part, and it is applied to the work a fraction above the centre line. While gravers of various sizes resemble each other, slide-rest tools are made in a number of special shapes according to the type of cut it is desired to produce. The slide-rest is used where very accurate work is required and is indispensible when quantity production is being undertaken.

A slide-rest can also be fitted with a vertical slide for cutting wheels. The blank to be cut is fixed on the centre line of the spindle of the lathe which can be locked by means of an arm fastened to the headstock. The driving pulley sometimes has a series of holes in its side for acting as a division plate, and sometimes a separate division plate can be fixed to the spindle on its outer end. The vertical slide contains a vertical spindle which carries the cutter at its lower end and a pulley at the upper. The height of the cutter can be adjusted to act

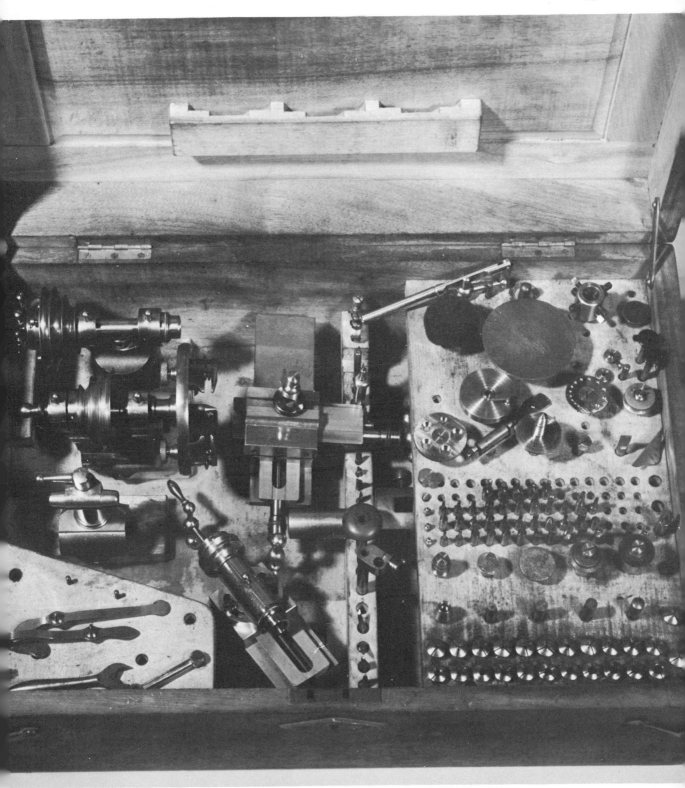

Some of the accessories supplied with a lorch lathe

either on the centre line for normal teeth, or obliquely when teeth of special shape, such as those for scapewheels, are being cut. The cutter is driven through the pulley by means of a belt, and after each cut the position of the blank is adjusted by means of the division plate and its locking arm as on a normal wheel-cutting engine.

Although the main advantage of the lathe is to perform turning by holding work at one end only, numerous attachments are provided for holding the work at its opposite end and are a necessity if the piece being worked on is of any length. A tailstock is provided which can accommodate runners of the type used in the turns or throw, and in addition it is possible to have a drilling attachment which, by means of a lever, can advance a drill into the centre of the work. Where it is desired to replace pivots, a rotating plate with a series of holes of different sizes is attached to the tail-stock, which can then be brought into line with the arbor being re-pivoted. The end of the arbor is supported by a conical depression concentric with the hole and the drill is advanced through the hole which it fits accurately, and therefore enters the work truly central. A similar plate with larger conical holes can be used for supporting large arbors such as clock-barrel arbors when they are being turned. Other accessories include a bell chuck with eight screws for holding pieces which are too large to fit into a normal split chuck. Opposite pairs of screws are operated on at the same time until the work runs absolutely true. Some lathes include small circular saws which are held on an arbor which is rotated by the main spindle; the work being held on a small table with a slot in it which fits onto the support for the toolrest. A series of sink cutters can be supplied for cutting depressions in watch plates to take motion wheels etc., the watchplate being held by the faceplate dogs while the sink cutter is mounted in the tailstock.

If it is desired to make part of an arbor of square section such as the winding stem of a keyless watch, this square is filed after the necessary turning has been done. A roller is held by the toolrest holder, and the file is partly supported by this roller and partly by the work, ensuring a perfectly flat cut. The arbor worked on is prevented from rotating by the arm on the headstock which secures the pulley when wheel-cutting. As soon as each flat is filed correctly, the arbor is rotated through 90° and the next cut made.

Some watch-maker's lathes have a tapered screw which can be fixed in the headstock to hold a piece of wood which is being turned. Wood turning does not normally come within the province of the watch-maker, but occasionally a piece has to be worked to form a support for a part which is being dealt with.

THE FINISHING OF PIVOTS

When pivots have been formed, their ends have to be finished and, in the very small sizes, a device is used similar to the disc with holes for supporting arbors when re-pivoting. In this case however, only a few holes are provided and as the diameter of the hole becomes smaller, the thickness of the metal in which it is drilled becomes less, allowing for a shorter pivot. This principle is also followed in the disc for re-pivoting. Pivot finishing in the larger sizes of arbor is accommodated by means of runners which are carried by the tailstock on the centre line of the work. These runners can be full length with different size holes at each end, for operating on different size pivots, or they can be quite short and mounted in the tapered end of another hollow runner which is secured in the tailstock.

The drive for the lathe was either by means of a hand wheel or a foot wheel. The latter had an advantage in allowing both hands to be free, but as all turning done previously required the left hand to work the hand wheel or the bow, the advantage would not have been so apparent to a man who was used to the old method. In more recent years the drive has been by electric motor with a variable resistance operated by the foot, but this suffers from the disadvantage of being very fast, and it is useful to be able to reduce speed by means of a countershaft.

5
THE WATCH

At the beginning of the eighteenth century, the typical English watch movement was rather thick with much decoration and comparatively large parts. It developed during the century by becoming thinner, the parts became smaller and it tended to have less decoration. In addition, several new escapements were invented which needed new techniques in their making. The average craftsman in any town could deal with repairs to the verge escapement, but one can imagine his dismay at being confronted with one of the new escapements for the first time.

THE VERGE ESCAPEMENT

The verge escapement had been in use since mechanical timekeepers first appeared. It never allowed the balance to swing with any freedom and the recoil caused extreme friction and so wasting power, it was sensitive to variations in driving force and needed a fusee to modify the pull of the mainspring. When the balance spring was applied to it about 1675–80, its performance greatly improved and Mr. Cecil Clutton has timed a watch of this period giving an error of only $1\frac{1}{2}$ minutes per day. As far as the needs of the time were concerned, this was more than adequate, but it was still far behind the performance of the long-case clock that could show the same amount of variation or less in a week.

Verge watch movements. *Above* late 17th century, *below* early 19th century.
Above left shows the arrangement of the scape wheel and the square stud
through which the balance spring is pinned

The chief troubles connected with a verge escapement were in its making. It required the scapewheel to revolve at right angles to the rest of the train and a separate bearing had to be mounted on the underside of the top plate to support its rear pivot, while the front pivot was accommodated in a hole in the 'pottance' or bracket that carried the lower pivot of the verge. These bearings had to allow for the adjustment of the scape arbor in relation to the verge, and endshake had to be almost entirely eliminated as it would cause variation in depth between the wheel and the pallets, and thereby affect the rate. The scapewheel itself was crown-shaped and needed a special appliance to make it and also the fourth wheel of the train had to be a contrate wheel to drive the scape pinion.

THE CYLINDER ESCAPEMENT

The first escapement produced in the eighteenth century to replace the verge was the cylinder which was invented by George Graham and based on an escapement which was patented by Tompion and others in 1695. The principle on which the cylinder worked was similar to that of Graham's dead-beat escapement for clocks where the faces on which the teeth lock were portions of the circumference of circles drawn from the centre of the pallet arbor. In the cylinder escapement, the cylinder itself is based on these circles, the teeth of the escape wheel impinging on the outer side of the entrance pallet and the inner side of the exit pallet when locking takes place. The edge of the cutaway portion of the cylinder received the impulse as the tooth passed, just as on the impulse faces of the Graham dead-beat escapement. The cylinder of the watch, however, moved with the balance and as it was necessary in a portable timekeeper that the balance had as wide a swing as possible to overcome disturbances which might affect the timekeeping or even stop the watch, the teeth were in contact with the locking faces for much longer and so caused friction. To allow for this extra rotation of the cylinder, the teeth of the scapewheel had to be mounted on stems, and the cylinder had to be cut away partly in the plane

of the wheel. This caused complications in the making of the wheel and made the cylinder weaker, but the great advantage which was gained over the verge, was that the scapewheel was in a plane parallel to that of the other train wheels and the contrate wheel could be replaced by a plain one. The elimination of the verge scapewheel paved the way for a thinner movement, but otherwise the cylinder movement was basically the same as the verge movement. The fusee and chain were retained, the decorated top plate and balance cock were as before and the layout of the train was unchanged. The pottance or cock that supported the lower end of the balance staff did not now carry the scapewheel pivot and so was simpler, but it needed a special adjustment so that the depthing of the scapewheel and cylinder could be controlled.

Cylinder movement by *Parkinson and Frodsham, London.* Early 19th century, this watch is very similar to the contemporary verge movement

Left a pocket chronomoter movement by *R. Westwood, Soho*. About 1840.
Right a Lever movement by *S. Norman, Soho*. About 1830

CUTTING CYLINDERS
AND SCAPEWHEELS

The earliest scapewheels were of brass and trouble was caused by the wearing of the steel cylinder, but the problem was overcome by making the cylinders out of ruby. Cutting a watch cylinder in a hard substance is a difficult task today for anyone except a specialist, and in the eighteenth century it must have been many times more so. The Swiss manufacturers later overcame the problem by making both the cylinder and scapewheel of steel and hardening them, also the wheel was of a somewhat different shape from the English wheel.

The cutting of a cylinder scapewheel involved the use of more than one cutter and could not very well be accomplished without using an engine with a division plate. The cylinder itself was drilled and had its outer surface finished in the turns, then the slit and clearance space would be made. At this stage it would be very frail and care would be needed when hardening. Plugs containing the top and bottom pivots were made in the turns, and the top one had a seating for the balance. The plugs were fitted into each end of the cylinder by careful tapping with a hammer and a hollow punch, a special form of punch with a

hooked end was evolved for removing them. A special piece of steel with different sized holes known as a 'stake' would be needed to support the cylinder while it was having the plugs fitted or removed.

WATCH JEWELLING

The use of jewels in watches was begun by Nicholas Facio, a Swiss, who endeavoured to get a patent in London in 1704. The idea was to provide a hard bearing for pivots that would resist wear. During the eighteenth century the practice was begun of mounting diamonds in the balance cocks of watches to act as an endstone and to prevent endshake of the balance arbor; this applied equally to the verge and the other escapements. The chief problem in jewelling was to drill a small accurate hole in a jewel to fit the pivot correctly. The stone was flattened on both sides by holding it against a rotating soft iron plate charged with diamond powder. When one side of the stone was flattened, it was reversed and the other side dealt with. After being cemented to a chuck, it was trued on the face and edge with a piece of black diamond set in a handle and then centred with a splint of the same substance and drilled halfway through. It was then reversed, the oilsink formed and the hole completed.

The process is a dirty one as the grinding surface must be supplied with plenty of water.

Watch jewelling remained a British speciality for years, while French makers continued to use metal bearings. As time went on, other pivots in the watch movement were provided with jewelled bearings even as far as the fusee, but here the speed of revolution was so slow that the need was doubtful.

THE LEVER ESCAPEMENT

The cylinder was the first break away from the verge, but it did little or nothing to harm the popularity of the latter. Verge watches continued to be made until about 1882, when the verge finishers died out, but naturally the last examples were extremely plain. The next new escapement to be invented in the eighteenth century was the lever which was put into a watch for Queen Charlotte by Thomas Mudge, its inventor, in 1769. The importance of this escapement was that the balance was detached for the greater part of its swing, making for much better timekeeping, but its inventor did not take great interest in it and it was left to others to develop later in the century. Mudge, like many other horologists of his time, was interested in developing the marine chronometer although the most outstanding work in this connection was done by Arnold and Earnshaw. They produced comparatively simple instruments compared with those made by their contemporaries and moreover, ones which were capable of being easily made in quantity, which was a feature of only secondary importance to the performance of the chronometer itself. The balances fitted to the chronometers of Arnold and Earnshaw were detached for almost the whole of their swing and only received impulse in one direction. This is no disadvantage on board ship where the chronometer is hung in gimbals in a special box, but when the chronometer escapement is used in a pocket watch it can be stopped by a sudden movement on the part of the wearer. In spite of this, many watches were made with the chronometer escapement over a long period from the end of the eighteenth century for customers who desired a timekeeper of extra precision.

A Duplex escapement movement of about 1830, it differs little in appearance from a verge movement but the jewelled bearing for the scape wheel is visible beside the lower arm of the balance. Two pivot holes lie between this bearing and the name bar

The Duplex movement with its outer cover to protect the works from dirt. They were mainly fitted between the late 17th and early 19th centuries; it is fastened by sliding the steel bar which fits under steel studs on opposite sides of the movement

Rack-lever movement, the large screw to the right of the balance adjusts the depth between the lever and the scape wheel

THE DUPLEX ESCAPEMENT

The really popular escapement for precision timekeeping in the late eighteenth century was the duplex. This was introduced by Dutertre about 1740 but it was only developed in Britain after about 1780 by Thomas Tyrer. The duplex escapement originally had two scape-wheels, but later the two sets of teeth were combined in one wheel which was naturally more difficult to make. The locking in the escapement was effected by long thin teeth impinging on what was virtually a cylinder of very small diameter. When the notch came round, the tooth advanced, and on the return swing of the balance it was allowed to escape. As the scapewheel continued its journey, one of the teeth nearer the centre would push aside a long finger attached to the balance staff and give the impulse. By the time the tooth had escaped from the end of the finger, another of the long teeth would be falling on the cylinder ready to repeat the cycle. The cylinder should theoretically be very small, but in practice it is

necessary to make it larger than the theoretical size to give it sufficient strength. Ruby was a favourite material but brought problems in working as the part was much smaller than on a cylinder watch and the slot was much finer. The small size of the roller would allow mis-locking as the balance pivot holes wore, which is one of the disadvantages of the duplex escapement. As it receives impulse in one direction only, it suffers like the chronometer escapement from being stopped by a sudden jerk; in spite of this, the duplex was a very popular escapement for a precision timekeeper at the end of the eighteenth century and the beginning of the nineteenth, it was superseded by the lever from about 1830–40 onwards.

THE RACK LEVER ESCAPEMENT

The next escapement to receive attention was the rack lever, introduced by Peter Litherland about 1790 following an idea by the Abbé Hautefeuille. This is virtually the Graham Dead-Beat Escapement used in a clock provided with a toothed sector on the end of its crutch that meshes with a pinion on the balance staff. As the balance vibrates, the pallets are moved to and fro and enable the scapewheel to advance and deliver impulse in so doing. This type of watch was a speciality of Liverpool and often included large jewels known as 'Liverpool Windows'. It was necessary to provide a fine adjustment of the depth between pallets and scapewheel, but otherwise there were few technical problems in the construction of a rack lever. In this escapement the balance was never detached and consequently timekeeping suffered, but the watches were fairly robust and a number were exported.

THE DECORATION OF WATCHES

As each new escapement appeared, watches generally were getting plainer. The most decoration was found on verges, but engraving gradually replaced the pierced work that was popular in the late seventeenth and early eighteenth centuries, and the newer styles, particularly rack levers, were very plain indeed by the standards of the time. As the new escapements became popular, it was necessary to provide longer and more flexible balance springs to allow for the greater movement of the balance and these balance springs were also fitted to verge movements. Mr. Cecil Clutton has found that these springs are less satisfactory with a verge escapement than the shorter and stiffer springs of the late seventeenth century.

An interesting feature of watch movements from the seventeenth through to the nineteenth centuries was the gilding of the plates after they had been finished. The earliest method was to dissolve gold in mercury, apply it to the part to be gilded and then heat the work until the mercury evaporated leaving a thin layer of gold behind. This process was also used for gilding clock dials and spandrels; it produced very poisonous fumes which meant an early death for the workers. The application of gold is now done by an electrical process, but the fashion of applying it to watch movements has died out. Its function was not entirely decorative; the gold protected the brass from corrosion and cleanliness is vital in a watch if it is to perform well. The gilding meant, however, that cleaning when it was done, had to be gentle and watch plates could not be cleaned using friction or abrasives as in the case of clock plates, for the gold surface could be easily removed.

Fullplate Lever movement by *Dent, Cockspur Street*. About 1870, it has a compensated balance

THE FULLPLATE LEVER ESCAPEMENT

After the various attempts to improve the lever escapement in the late eighteenth and early nineteenth centuries, the design settled down in the 1830s in the form in which it established a world-wide reputation. The layout of the train was still the same as in other fullplate watches except that the third wheel now came near the dial side of the watch, and its arbor was on the escapement side of the fourth wheel. This change had gradually evolved during the eighteenth century and even verge watches were made with the new arrangement. Instead of the third and fourth arbors being supported by the bottom plate, their pivots were carried by a removable bar which was screwed to the plate on the dial side, and thus allowed the third wheel and fourth pinion to work in the thickness of the plate. The fusee was retained, but usually carried a maintaining ratchet that would keep the watch going for a minute or so while the power was removed when winding took place. Usually two pillars came between the barrel and fusee and helped to make the replacement of the chain more difficult. The chain was very fine and the fusee very flat, for everything was being done to make the watch as thin as possible. Very little of the barrel arbor projected through the ratchet on the front plate for setting up the mainspring and it was difficult to get a key on the square when replacing the chain. An old trick was to push the ratchet into position with a piece of pegwood held in the teeth when the mainspring had been set up half a turn.

The fullplate lever watch enjoyed a great reputation for accuracy but it was a terrible

62

thing to strip and assemble. In spite of its faults of design, large numbers of them were made, for by that time the factory system, which had been growing up since Tompion's time, was well established and no one gave any consideration to trying to create a watch that was easy to repair. A workman would spend several hours on cleaning such a watch and receive only a few shillings for his labour, but he was handling the type week in and week out and took the work in his stride.

DEVELOPMENT OF
MASS PRODUCTION

The various new escapements which needed fine tools for their making, all helped to increase the number of watches produced in factories and tended to make the individual craftsman more of a retailer and repairer and less of a maker. The equipment needed for manufacturing was expensive and only justifiable for quantity production rather than one-off jobs. Another development in the factory system was in the manufacture of chains for fusees. These had been made by specialist craftsmen in various places during the eighteenth century or else imported, but a certain

The front plate of a Lever movement showing a separate bar for carrying the 3rd and 4th pivots

Robert Cox of Christchurch, Hants., conceived the idea of using children from the local workhouse to produce fusee chains. Workhouse labour was eventually discontinued, but factories were established in the town and a number of outworkers were associated with them—women who produced chains in their own homes and then took them to the factory for testing and finishing. The making of the chains has been described in a fascinating book by Mr. Allen White. Special dies were used which cut the links from steel strip and at the same time perforated the two rivet holes; the operator would pick up a link on a wire by threading it through a hole, and then add two more links. The centre link would face in the opposite direction to the two outer ones. The wire was cut at each end, making a 'burr' and then the links were riveted together, not so tightly as to bind and not so loosely that they might come apart. The projecting centre link was then placed between another pair and the three riveted together and so on until the chain was complete. The special hooks for the fusee and barrel ends of the chains were then added and the chain tempered and polished.

FOREIGN COMPETITION

The popularity of the lever watch was probably brought about by the development of railways. The increase in travel necessitated watches which were accurate enough to enable their owners to catch trains and also be less sensitive than the chronometer or duplex watches with their danger of stopping as the result of a sudden movement. Manufacture in this country concentrated on centres such as Clerkenwell, Birmingham, Coventry and Lancashire. During the nineteenth century, Swiss watches were imported in increasing numbers and many of these had bar movements where every wheel was supported by its own bracket or 'cock', making for ease in stripping and assembling and in addition saving time and cost by dispensing with the fusee. Many had the cylinder escapement which meant one cock fewer than when this layout is used with a lever watch as the cock for the pallets is absent. After the American Civil War, American watches were also imported into Britain, mostly Walthams, which were fullplate watches like the usual English models but which omitted the fusee.

The seriousness of foreign competition did not have much effect on British manufacturers. They continued to produce their old models using a great deal of hand work, and it is hardly surprising that the industry was practically dead by 1900. A slight concession occurred in certain instances where watches originally intended to have fusees, were actually produced with dummy barrels the same size as the one actually containing the mainspring. The dummy meshed with the normal barrel and had no function other than to occupy the space between the plates where the fusee would normally have been situated.

The import of foreign watches helped the man at the bench in that supplies of spare parts were available. Previously, if a part in a hand-made watch was broken, it was necessary for the repairer to make a replacement. The imported factory-made watches were built up of identical parts that were readily inter-changeable. This was not the case even with later English watches. The writer once acquired a number of ex-railway watches bearing the name of a well-known London retailer. An identical movement was also seen bearing the name of another firm, indicating that the movement was factory-made and engraved with the name of the retailer to order. When it came to cannibalising the movements, many of the larger parts such as barrels were readily interchangeable, but the escapements were all individually fitted.

KEYLESS WATCHES

A new complication was added in the nine-teenth century by the introduction of keyless work. Among the earliest was that of Thomas Prest of Chigwell, who was foreman at Arnold's chronometer factory; Prest's arrange-ment was not used for setting the hands which had to be done independently. In a later method this was accomplished by pressing a stud which moved a rocking bar and put the

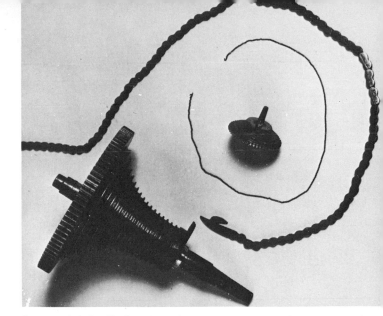

Fusee and chain. Clock and watch sizes compared

winding button in gear with the motion work at the same time as it disengaged the connec-tion between the button and the mainspring. Other methods required the button to be pulled out or pushed in to set the hands; a further method, found mostly in American watches, had a small lever at the side of the dial that had to be pulled out to enable the hands to be set. This was really a retrograde step as it involved opening the glass, but the idea was used for railroad watches in the U.S.A. to ensure that the hands could not be altered accidentally while the watch was in the wearer's pocket.

The chief objection to keyless work was caused by the fusee. As a fusee watch runs down, the fusee arbor rotates, and if this were connected to the winding button by the keyless work, the rotation of the button against the side of the pocket might cause interference with the going of the watch. Methods were devised to overcome this difficulty, but the keyless watch did not really become popular until the going barrel was well established. Here the barrel arbor rotates when the watch is wound, but remains stationary as the spring runs down and consequently no difficulty arises from carrying the watch in the pocket. The winding gear involved the making of two or more toothed wheels, cut in steel to give strength and durability, plus various levers and springs all of which had to work smoothly with each other and stand up to repeated use. It added to the work and time spent on stripping and assembling and rendered the sale of watch keys unnecessary. For these reasons, it was a disadvantage to the trade although an advantage to the owner of the watch.

By the end of the nineteenth century, the usual type of watch sold was a three-quarter plate without a fusee and fitted with keyless work, although a number of keywound watches were still available. The lever escapement was popular, but a large number of cylinder watches were imported from Switzerland and they gave reasonable service. Following the lead given by Roskopf, a number of cheap watches were produced provided with pin pallet lever escapements and mostly without jewelling. The marketing of these led the way to dispensing with repairs and discarding the watch in favour of a new one when serious trouble developed.

Below, left Swiss bar movement with cylinder escapement
right fullplate watch movement by the Waltham Watch Co. U.S.A. of about 1890

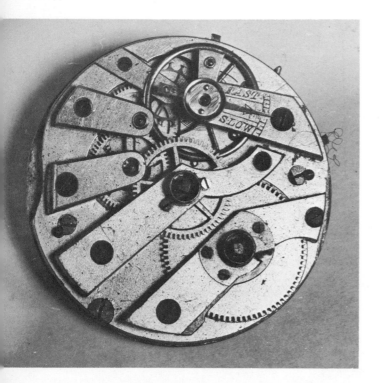

6
CLOCKS
IN THE
NINETEENTH
CENTURY

The nineteenth century is in many ways the most interesting period of our study. Not only were there more types of British clock and watch on the market than before, but many foreign types were being imported which added to the task of the clock and watch-maker, requiring him to gain wider knowledge and experience. As a compensation for this, many spare parts could be obtained from the factories in a finished condition.

EUROPEAN CLOCKS

The earliest imports into this country in the realm of clocks were the weight-driven wall clocks with wooden frames made in the Black Forest. These clocks were found in many homes as the development of the factory system rendered it more necessary for families to know the correct time instead of relying on the chimes of a neighbouring church. Many firms in various towns arranged to import these clocks and they were not only sold in shops but also hawked in the streets by travel-ling salesmen. Mr. T. A. Camerer Cuss has some old documents from his firm relating to a consignment of Black Forest clocks sent from Hamburg to London in 1816 and to another consignment which not only included finished clocks but also spare dials, chains and hands. The Black Forest clock was a sturdy and reliable performer and usually only stopped when completely gummed up with congealed oil and dirt. A clean-up would leave them as sound as ever and apart from the occasional rebushing required, few repairs were neces-sary.

About 1810 clocks began to be produced in factories in France and eventually large numbers of movements were exported to this country either in cases or else on their own ready to be fitted into English-made cases on arrival. The French type of movement was one of the best which were produced com-mercially, and its size and finish made it a nearer approach to watchwork than any other type of clock, it required careful handling during assembly. The pinions and pallets of these clocks were often glass-hard which gave very durable service but required extra care

Left a typical
French striking
movement. At the
top is the *Brocot*
pendulum
suspension
adjusted by a key
on the small square
over the figure XII

Below French-
wheel blanks
mounted on arbors
and ready for
cutting

when being handled. French movements were extensively used for the better quality clocks in England in the nineteenth century and were in general production till 1914. The usual reason for their being brought to a repairer was cleaning, but new mainsprings were sometimes required and also new suspension springs for the pendulums when the *Brocot* type of regulation was used. The typical French clock was housed in a heavy marble case, which meant that it was not often moved. This was a good feature from a timekeeping point of view but meant that regulation, by means of a rating nut at the bottom of the pendulum, was difficult. The *Brocot* suspension is gripped by a pair of jaws which can be raised or lowered by means of a small square over the figure 12 which is operated by a small key, and this gives a very fine degree of regulation without the clock having to be moved.

If it should happen that a French clock broke some of the teeth in its wheels, blank wheels already mounted on pinions were sold which could be brought to the correct diameter and cut as necessary. Spare suspension springs and their accompanying mechanism were also sold and this enabled many of the older French clocks which formerly had silk suspensions, to have these replaced by the more reliable spring suspensions. The repairer would be required to drill the necessary holes in the plates and dial, and finish the parts to suit the movement being operated on. The basic French movement changed very little during the century in which it was exported to Britain, and repairers everywhere would know it and have the appropriate material in stock to undertake the necessary repairs.

THE AMERICAN OG CLOCKS

After 1842, the Black Forest clocks were gradually driven off the market by the American OG weight-driven clocks and later by spring-driven clocks from the same country. These clocks had a variety of cases, it being the practice of the factories to give each style a name, but the movements although differing in detail, were all of the same basic pattern. The plates were stamped out of

rolled sheet brass and the wheels were made likewise except that a stiffening ring was also produced by the die. The lifting pieces in the clocks that had striking mechanisms, were made of wire and consequently tended to be springy and sometimes refused to lock properly. These clocks usually had a wire that could be pulled or pushed to release the striking and get the number of hours sounded in step with the hands once more.

The American striking movement was a complicated piece of mechanism to assemble, as the lifting pieces were often threaded between the arbors, and as they had springs formed from pieces of fine wire coiled round

Typical Black Forest Wall clock of about 1830

American OG clock by the Waterbury Clock Co.
About 1870

Black Forest wall clock with circular dial made
specially for the British market. The name on the dial
is that of the importer, *G. Spiegelhalter & Co.*
Whitechapel Road of about 1840

them they would often spring out of place
during assembly and perhaps disarrange some
of the other parts. Later American clocks,
such as the model produced by the Ansonia
company in the 1880s and 1890s, had their
striking arranged so that the wheel which
carried the cam for locking also bore the pins
which lifted the hammer, and this meant that
there was no need to worry about the relationship between the locking and the position of
the hammer tail when assembling the clock,
as on other models. It was only necessary to
make sure that the warning pin was in such a
position that the train was able to have a short
run when warning took place. The French
movements had some of the pivots supported
by a separate cock which was fastened by a
screw and two steady pins, and this enabled
the striking train to be set correctly with less
difficulty.

WATCH IMPORTS

Watches were also imported, mainly from
Switzerland, and their simplicity and cheap-
ness had a marked effect on the sales of the
British types of watch. Certain people were
alarmed at the situation by the middle of the
century, but in general little notice was taken
by the trade and it is not surprising that
British watch manufacture was practically
dead by the end of the century. After 1860,
the American factories such as Waltham began
exporting to this country as well, and further
weakened the market for the British product.
The making of watches by individual craftsmen was rare by the nineteenth century and
we have already seen that the leading London
clockmakers were having their movements
produced in specialist workshops in the
eighteenth century. By the early nineteenth,
most provincial clockmakers were getting
their movements from Birmingham and the
only 'making' they did was to finish spare
parts from partly prepared material. If a man
worked in a comparatively inaccessible spot
he would be more obliged to make his spare
parts from raw metal that had not been
previously prepared. The range of equipment
was greater even than can be obtained today.

In a sense, the workman was in a less fortunate position. A hundred years previously the number of types of clock and watch that he had to deal with were more limited, and the number of spare parts that he would have been called upon to make were much fewer. As the types multiplied, so did the number of parts, and the repairer's ingenuity had to be greater, with the invention of the watch-maker's lathe about 1860 his capacity for producing more work in less time was increased, but of course such machines were expensive and not everyone could afford them. Many men were very conservative and would not use them, maintaining quite rightly that the turns with work turned on its own centres was true, whereas the lathe with its chucks was not necessarily so. In the field of mass production, the lathe was an absolute necessity.

ADDITIONAL BUSINESS ACTIVITIES

In the country, the watch and clockmaker did not spend all his time on horological repairs. John Neve Masters describes in his reminiscences of his father's shop about 1850, that all kinds of work were brought in to be done. The vicar's wife sometimes wanted a tongue scraper which was made out of a piece of old watch spring and on one occasion, a customer came in to have his false teeth repaired. This job was coldly declined as it was considered sinful in those days to have false teeth. Apparently wooden legs were not sinful! Masters also tells us that customers would often come in with a verge watch that was gaining furiously and be told that they could have it back in an hour. The trouble was simply that two turns of the balance spring had got caught in the curb pins: a matter that only required a minute or two to put right; the celebrated watch of Captain Cuttle in *Dombey & Son* apparently suffered from this fault.

A country watch and clock business would probably not provide enough work to give its owner a living and consequently he would be compelled to seek a side-line for his activities. Apart from small repairs to metal objects, he would carry on some sort of business such as

Shop dial. James Bannister, Princes Street, Leicester Square. About 1850

that of ironmonger or general dealer. A paper found in a long-case clock bearing the name of R. Blakeborough of Otley, Yorkshire, 1822–41, gives a complete picture of such an undertaking.

I, R. Blakeborough, Watch and Clockmaker, Jeweller, Silversmith and Ironmonger, grateful for the liberal support which he has experienced for many years, begs leave to inform the inhabitants of Otley, and its environs, that he continues to sell the following articles at reduced prices: Watches, plain and patent lever Horizontal and clocks of all descriptions, Gold watch chains, seals and keys, Gold broaches, ear rings and hoops, Necklaces and wedding rings of standard gold, Gold, gilt and silver snaps, Gilt and jet necklaces, black ear rings, broaches and coloured beads of all kinds, silver, gilt steel and leather purses, gilt watch chains, seals and keys, gold, gilt and silver clips and buckles.

Fifes, flutes, violin strings etc.
Walking sticks and canes,
Mahogany swing looking glasses,
Do. hanging do.
Pier Glasses in gilt frames,
Sykes patent powder flasks,
Shot belts
Guns, double and single barrel
Pistols and Flints
Ladies' Pelisse clasps, silver gilt or steel
Spring Roasting Jacks
Brass and Japanned Cases
Copper Scales and Beams
Beams of all kinds
Brass and polished steel fenders
Green Fenders with brass tops and balls
Kitchen do.
Polished and common fire irons
Box and solid irons
Bellows

Brushes, Broom heads and hearth brushes
Flat and Round Witheners
Best Painters, Stove and Shoe Brushes
Bottle Brushes
Hair and Tooth do. etc. etc.
Black and bright augers, gimblets
Do. and do. Hammers
Mason's trowels
Smoothing Planes
Jack Planes
Short Trying do.
Long Trying do.
Bead do.
Nails of all sorts
Hand Panel and Ripping Saws
Dovetail and Tenon do.
Cast Steel Chisels and Gouges
Do. Garden and Turnip hoes
Cast Steel Plane Irons
All kinds of attire for Carpenters, Joiners etc.
Weights, Butchers
Tea Trays, paper and japanned
Tea Pots, Table and Tea Spoons
Tea Caddies and Tea Chests
Japanned Bread Baskets, Waiter and Chamber Candlesticks
Brass and Iron Candlesticks
Knives with Ivory Handles and Carvers to match
Dessert do. do.
Knives with Stag and Pressed handles
Pocket and Penknives
Scissors of all kinds
Lamp Black
Emery
Crocus
Pumice Stone etc.
Rasps and Files of various kinds
Locks and Hinges of all kinds
Stringing and shells for inlaying

Commodes
Knobs, escutcheons, locks etc.
Hinges and Screws
Bells
Curtain Pins
Rings
Brass Nails etc.

Castings
Ranges, Stoves, Ovens and Boilers
Hearth Grates
Pots and Pans
Frying Pans etc.

In addition to the above list, R.B. has very recently received a fresh supply of hardware, Jewellery, Silver and Plated Goods too numerous for insertion. R.B. Cleans and carefully repairs clocks and watches of every description also weather glasses, bottle jacks, silver plate etc. The best prices given for old gold and silver.

EDWARD BAINES. PRINTER. LEEDS.

A COUNTRY CLOCKMAKER'S WEEK

By about 1860, a country clockmaker's week would possibly be spent something like this:
Monday He rose at dawn and lit the fire in the workshop. He dismantled an 8-day long-case movement for overhaul which had been collected from a customer the previous week. 8 a.m. breakfast after which he cleaned the parts of the 8-day clock in a solution of soap and ammonia to remove all grease and brightened the parts with rottenstone and oil. He cleaned the pivot holes in the plates by twirling a pointed piece of pegwood in them until it emerged clean and cleaned the larger holes by pulling a strip of leather through them. The end of the bench had several strips of different diameters nailed to it for this

purpose. All pivots were polished in the throw, and where they were badly cut he re-shaped them with a graver till they were parallel once more and then polished them. When some of the pivots were reduced in size the holes needed rebushing. This was done by means of a special bushing rod, i.e. a brass rod with a hole drilled through the centre. The old pivot hole was opened with a broach until the bush almost fitted, then the latter was tapped home to a good fit and the hole in the centre opened with another broach until the pivot almost fitted. Work then continued with a smooth broach that hardened the inside of the hole and left a polish which helped to overcome friction.

The fly pinion of this clock was very worn and a new one was necessary. This was made as described in Chapter 3 and when it ran smoothly it was hardened and finished. The pallets were not very worn and only required their faces smoothed and polished. New gut lines were inserted, and after the knots had been tied the ends were seared with a piece of iron that was heated in the workshop fire. This also serves to heat pieces of steel for hardening and to heat soldering irons etc. A kettle is kept on the fire for a supply of hot water for washing etc., but at this period is not used for making tea as it is expensive. During the winter the clockmaker might take a glass of spirits and hot water in the evening, but his normal drink was probably ale.

If he required heat in small quantities for such jobs as heating small drills, he used a spirit lamp. This could have its flame directed or intensified by a mouth blowpipe. His source of light possibly was a colza oil lamp with a clockwork pump. Mineral oil was not yet much in use; the first oil well was drilled in Pennsylvania in 1858. Domestic light at this time was usually supplied by candles.

As soon as all the parts of the clock were cleaned and repaired the clock was re-assembled. With the skill born of long practice and after the striking train had been adjusted so that the train locked just after the hammer tail had been released by a pin, the plates were pinned together and the strike-control mechanism behind the dial was pinned in place. After

Spirit lamp with two sticks of shellac

oiling had been done, the dial and hands were put on and the clock was mounted on a testing frame with the weights and pendulum hung on and set running.

It was late afternoon by now and dusk was falling. During the day, various interruptions would have occurred by customers coming into the shop to leave watches for repair or to make a simple purchase like a watchkey or to have a new glass inserted in a watch. As the clockmaker was now working by artificial light, he used a globe of water to concentrate the rays on the bench. Between 8 and 9 p.m. he would put up the shutters and retire to his living room for supper and bed.

Tuesday The clockmaker got up as early as before, but he dressed himself in his best suit and went over the way to the barber to get a shave as today is winding day at the various big houses in the neighbourhood. He carried a small bag of tools with him to deal with any small repairs that could be done on the spot and a set of keys of different sizes. There are three large houses in the district which he attends. At two of them he wound the long-case clock in the hall, the French clock in the drawing room and the solid English clocks in the dining room and library. The third house was larger than the other two and possessed long-case clocks in the hall and on the landing.

The library and the owner's study also contained clocks that had to be wound, as well as the small striking turret clock at the stables which has to be attended to. This clock got a little oil and was wiped down at every visit. In addition to winding all the clocks, he checked their going against a watch he carried with him. This is a fullplate duplex watch with a very close rate, and before visiting the various houses he went to the railway station to get the correct time, which is telegraphed from London at 10 a.m. each day. It is only a few years since that Greenwich Mean Time has been used throughout the country and previously every place used its local time. If a town does not have a railway station, it is necessary to correct the watch by means of a sundial together with an equation table for finding the difference between mean and solar time.

If any of the clocks showed alarming variations in their rate, he examined the clock carefully and suggested to the owner that it was perhaps time to have it cleaned. If the owner agreed, the clockmaker would take the clock back to the shop and begin work as soon as possible for regular customers could not be kept waiting. At their midday meal, the clockmaker and his wife finished up the last of a leg of mutton which had been eaten hot on Sunday, and he took the bone back to the workshop and put it on the fire. The fire burnt the bone white and destroyed all the remaining fatty matter, and when it was ready it was removed from the fire and allowed to cool. It was then used for cleaning the brushes that are used for polishing the parts of watches and clocks after they have been cleaned. The burnt bone absorbed dirt and grease and helped to get a good shine on the brass.

During the clockmaker's absence, the grocer brought in his shop dial because it kept stopping. The trouble here is congealed oil; the choice of oil is rather limited as only vegetable or animal oils were available and they usually caused corrosion where they came into contact with the brass and produced a green residue which had to be removed regularly. Clocks at that time really did need cleaning frequently. Under modern conditions, the air is cleaner and oils remain fluid for longer, but back in the 1860s with gas or oil lamps for illumination and open coal fires for heating, the air was less favourable to fine mechanisms. A farmer also left a large silver verge watch because he dropped it on the stone floor of his kitchen and broke the verge. The clockmaker decided to do the watch first as his hands were clean and he had not been doing heavy work during the morning. If he had been cleaning a really dirty clock, the sensitivity of his hands would have been dulled and he would not have worked so well.

The verge for a watch is a long thin axis with two tiny pallets on it approximately at right angles to each other. The axis is extended above the top pallet to allow for the seating of the balance and the balance spring collet. It is much too frail an object to be worked on in the turns by itself, so a length of pegwood is taken slightly shorter than the new verge so that the ends can protrude, and a segment is cut out of it throughout its length. The verge is laid in the bottom of the groove left by this process and the cut-out piece is replaced and a ferrule fastened over it to hold the whole assembly together. The verge can now be worked on in the turns, and after measuring the total length the pivots can be turned with pivoting runners as described previously. The balance and balance spring are mounted on a brass collet which rests on the top pallet. A piece of brass is drilled and broached to a push-on fit and soldered in position on the verge and the seats for the balance-spring collet and the balance are turned using the verge as a centre. The seatings are cut true by this method. The angle of the pallets can be altered by holding one end of the verge in a pinvice and heating the centre of it by means of a flame directed by a blowpipe. A piece of pegwood is slit and fastened on the lower pallet and so held that its weight causes the verge to twist in the appropriate direction until the pallets are at the correct angle to each other. After the balance and balance spring have been fixed, the verge is tried in the watch, and the pallets are found to be a shade too long. The extreme edges are rubbed off by a stone and a smoother stone is used to smooth them when

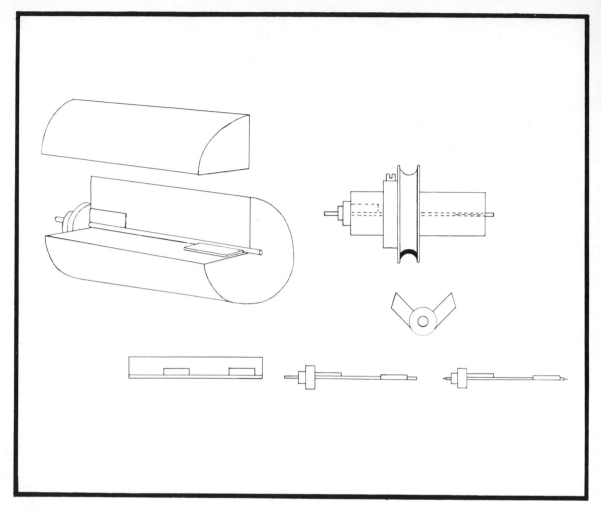

Making a Verge.
Above left A piece of pegwood is split lengthwise and one quarter removed. The verge is laid in the groove and the segment replaced and held in position by a ferrule, *above right*. The ends of the verge can now be supported in the turns and the whole assembly is stiff enough to resist the action of the turning tool. *Below left* a sheet of steel with the verge body and pallets marked. This is then filed to shape and twisted so that the pallets are at right angles. This is done by warming the centre of the verge. *Below centre* shows the brass collet for the balance and balance spring mounted on the verge. *Below right* the finished verge with the pivots and collet turned. *Centre right* shows the position of the pallets in the last two drawings with the pallet nearest to the collet on the right

they are the correct size. The pivot holes for the scapewheel are slightly adjustable to give a good action to the escapement.

Rough verges of various sizes were obtainable from dealers, but some repairers made their own out of old pieces of mainspring. It is possible to try the verge in the watch without fitting the balance spring, and if all is in order the minute hand of the watch should move about 25 to 30 minutes when the watch has been going an hour, as the balance spring makes the action about twice as fast.

The grocer's dial clock was then cleaned in the same way as the long-case clock, but as the line connecting the fusee and barrel had frayed, a new one was inserted. The fusee and main wheel are held together by a sliding plate which is fastened by a small screw. Once this is removed, the fusee and main wheel can be taken apart and the line cut, thus causing the old knot to fall out of the hole in the base of the fusee, a new line is inserted and the knot seared. The fusee is now reassembled after the clickwork has been checked; this fits into a space cut in the face of the main wheel and is normally hidden by the fusee itself. If the fusee is not taken to pieces, the clickwork can get neglected and may cause an accident later. The new gut line is wrapped round the fusee until all grooves are filled and the line is cut allowing about 9 in. extra. It is fastened into the barrel by means of three holes in the rim which are so arranged that the tighter the pull on the line, the tighter the end is gripped in a loop. The end of the line is seared as an extra precaution to prevent it running back.

The hole taking the centre pivot at the rear has a great deal of pressure to withstand and has been worn oval, so the clockmaker put a new bush in. After he had made the pivot hole the correct size by cutting and smoothing broaches, he made a small chamfer on the outer side to help it retain the oil. The clock was then re-assembled and the line wound on the barrel. The scapewheel was wedged by a piece of pegwood and the clock wound using a key on the fusee square. The line was guided onto the fusee as necessary, and when this was done, the pegwood was removed. If the train ran smoothly, the pallets were then inserted and the movement replaced in its case

Balance spring and balance with broken verge, plus rough verges ready for finishing

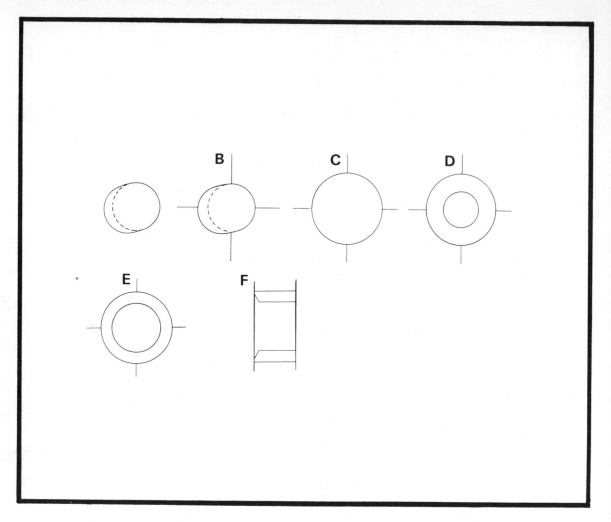

Inserting a Bush. (The heavy line shows the shape of the worn hole and the dotted its original size)
[B] lines are scratched so as to find the original centre
[C] the hole is filed on the opposite side to the wear to equalise it, it is then broached to a larger diameter
[D] a bush is inserted and hammered in tight
[E] the centre hole in the bush is drilled out to the original size of the hole
[F] the new bush is chamfered on the outer side to make an oil sink

for testing. The hands of the clock showed signs of rust in places so he cleaned them with a fine emery buff and 'blued' them again by gently warming them over the spirit lamp. This is a delicate operation and it takes a lot of practice to get an even colour all over.

Various customers brought clocks and watches into the shop during the time that the repairs were carried out but it was late in the evening and the clockmaker put up the shutters and retired to his living room.

Wednesday He spent the morning on one or two routine watch repairs. A lady's Geneva watch wanted a new mainspring, another needed a new glass and another farmer had brought in a big silver pair-cased verge watch

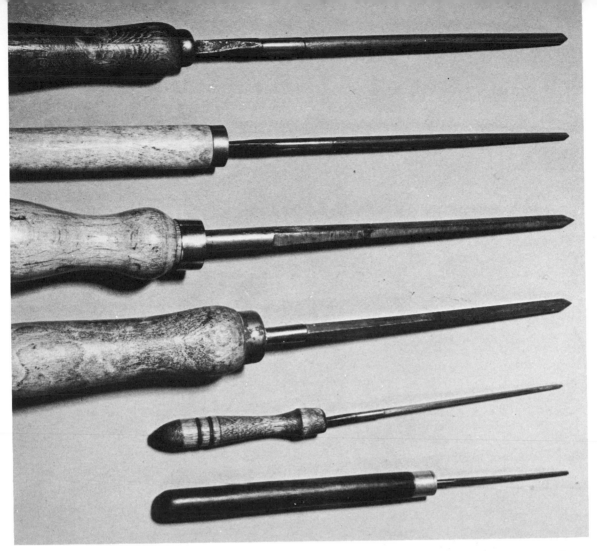

Two smoothing broaches and four cutting broaches

Silver Verge watch of about 1840. This type was often known as a 'Farmer's Verge'

which only needed cleaning—the verge itself was intact.

He removed the movement from the case by releasing the catch below the figure VI and then pushed out the pin over figure XII. This also fastened the bezel and glass and the case is put away in a drawer until it is required. The hands are removed by a pair of tools resembling a miniature burglar's jemmy. These are inserted under the boss of the hand and take a bearing on the dial, which is protected by small pieces of paper while the operation is in progress. The movement is then laid dial downwards and the pins holding the dial pillars removed after which the dial comes off and the hour and minute wheels can be taken off and put on one side. The cannon pinion is removed by holding it with pliers and twisting it off. Care is needed not to bend the centre arbor or fracture will result. A small piece of pegwood is then put between the crossings of the contrate wheel and the balance cock unscrewed. The point in the plate where the end of the balance spring comes, is marked with a scratch to facilitate replacing the spring in its correct position. The balance spring is then unpinned and led out of its stud by tweezers after which the balance and verge can be lifted out. As soon as the verge is free the train will begin to run, but it is almost immediately stopped by the piece of pegwood inserted into the crossings of the contrate wheel. The train can be allowed to run down under supervision and then the odd half turn of the mainspring can be let down by releasing the ratchet on the front plate while holding the barrel arbor firmly with tongs. The chain is then loose and can be removed.

The bar holding the barrel in position is removed and also the pins holding the top plate, after which the wheels can be taken out. After the decorative work holding the regulator in position on the top plate has been removed, the parts of the watch are all ready for cleaning. Only a dry brush is used for this purpose and it is frequently rubbed on a burnt bone to clean it and to absorb the grease. The cleaning process must not be too violent as the layer of gilding might be damaged. The holes are pegged out with small pieces of pointed

pegwood until the wood emerges from the hole in clean condition.

Re-assembling is done in the reverse order and the chain is replaced by hooking the appropriate end to the barrel and rotating the latter by the square end of the arbor which protrudes through the front plate and carries the ratchet. As the last turn of chain approaches the barrel, the hook at the fusee end is engaged and a further half turn of the barrel arbor gives the necessary tension to the spring and keeps the chain taut when the watch is run down. The click can then be engaged and screwed tight. During re-assembly the parts are held with tissue paper to protect the newly cleaned watch from the fingers. While the parts are on the bench, they are covered with an old wineglass to protect them from dust and damage.

When the re-assembly was complete, it was customary to put a watch paper into the back of the outer case which acted as an advertisement for the business. The papers were printed locally and were on square sheets of paper. The printed part of each sheet had to be cut out with scissors and a number of small cuts made round the edge to enable it to fit into the curved case of the watch. Watch papers were getting old-fashioned by then. They were useful in the days of the old-fashioned pair case watch but the more modern cases did not leave room for them and although there were still plenty of the old cases about, they were

Watch papers

Brushes for cleaning brass, they are frequently rubbed on the lump of chalk shown

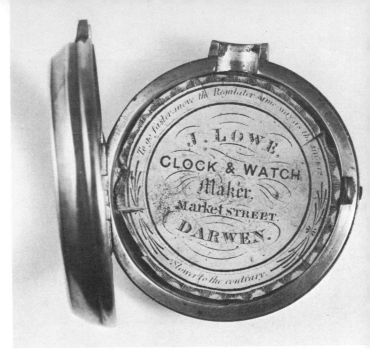

Watch paper inserted in the outer case of a watch

increasingly being supplanted by more modern watches, in particular the fullplate lever, the back of the case of which opened like a door to reveal the winding square in a hole in the inner dome. However the glass had to be opened to set the hands. The lever watch was very much thinner than the verge and was consequently more difficult to work with. However they quickly gained popularity and the clockmaker has had plenty of experience of the type.

He had to deal with one today as a commercial traveller staying at the local inn, had knocked his watch off the bedside table breaking the balance staff, so a new one had to be made for it. The staff of a fullplate lever is much simpler than a modern staff which includes the seat for the balance. It is virtually a straight rod with specially formed pivots at the ends and is derived from the old verge. The balance and its spring are supported by a small brass collet near one end, and the roller which carries the pin which engages with the lever, is a push-on fit at the other end. Sometimes the balance spring is below the balance as on the older verge watches and cannot be removed until the roller has been taken off, but later watches have the spring above the balance as in a modern watch.

The old staff is used as a guide for making the new one. The roller is removed by holding it in a pinvice and it can then be twisted off. The balance is riveted on to the brass collet, and before it can be removed the balance spring must be taken away; this is done by inserting a wedge-shaped piece of steel into the slot in the spring collet which slightly enlarges its diameter and allows it to be lifted off the brass collet on the staff. The staff is then mounted in the turns with a suitable ferrule and the riveting cut away with a very sharp graver, the balance can then be removed. The new staff is made from a piece of steel slightly longer and thicker than the old one; it is pointed at each end by being held in a pinvice and rotated on a wood block with slots in its edge. The points are formed with a file pushed forward as the top edge of the staff rotates towards the operator. When the points have been made, the staff is then mounted in runners in the turns with female centres and fitted with a suitable ferrule. The ferrule is driven by a horsehair in the bow, as it is stronger than a cotton thread and does not tend to fray. The staff is turned to the same diameter as the old one and the correct length marked. When the sides of the staff are parallel, it is smoothed and polished in the turns and

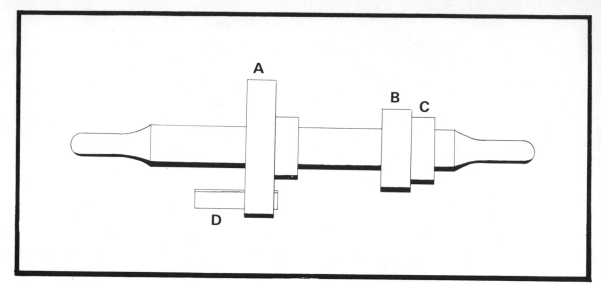

The Staff of a Fullplate Lever Watch.
[A] is the roller containing the impulse pin (D) which enters the fork of the lever,
[B] is the seating for the balance spring collet and [C] is the seating for the balance

the special pivots are formed. The diameter is, of course, checked while work is in progress to ensure that the roller will be firmly held by a push-on fit.

The collet for the balance is formed from a small piece of brass which is drilled and broached so that it is a tight fit on the staff. The seatings for the balance and its spring are turned, leaving enough metal to allow the balance to be riveted, and the collet is then adjusted to its correct position and soldered into place. The balance can then be riveted on, using a stake and a hollow punch. The hole in the stake which is chosen just allows the staff to enter and no more, giving plenty of support to the collet. The pivots are formed with the aid of a hollow runner, and the ends have to be rounded and polished to minimise friction between the staff and the endstones. When the pivots are completed, the staff is tried in the watch for correct height, and if all is in order, the balance spring and the roller are put in place and the staff can be put into position once more.

His afternoon was occupied with cleaning and rebushing a thirty-hour long-case clock with countwheel striking, and this was dealt with in much the same way as the eight-day clock which he repaired on Monday.

Thursday Thursday was market day in this town, and consequently the clockmaker was busy attending to customers who come to the shop with large or small repairs. Watch glasses had to be inserted, keys supplied, bracelets, pendants or other pieces of jewellery received small repairs, and one or two items such as watch chains were sold. The bank was open today, and he made a hurried visit to deposit some of the money he had taken since the last market day. Towards the end of the day, some of the small farmers and market gardeners called at the shop after concluding their business and left work to be done or collected jobs left previously. Some of these were paid for in kind, such as butter, eggs or a fowl, for business still had affinities with the old system of barter and the town and the country were still much closer together.

Friday After the bustle of market day, Friday was usually somewhat quieter. The clockmaker was able to make one or two business calls on his own account, he visited the saddler to pick up some strips of leather for cleaning large holes in clock plates and a bottle of neatsfoot oil for keeping gut lines supple. He also got a fresh supply of soap and ammonia from the ironmonger and more spirit for his lamp. A visit to the dressmaker produced a

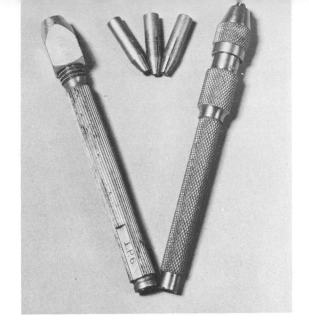

Right pinvices and chucks. The tool is hollow so that a piece of wire can be threaded right through it when making a number of pins. As each pin is finished it is cut off and then the wire is pushed through the tool for the next so saving reloading time

Below staking tool and punches. The rod mounted in the tool is used to locate accurately the hole in the base which is in line with the tube which guides the punches

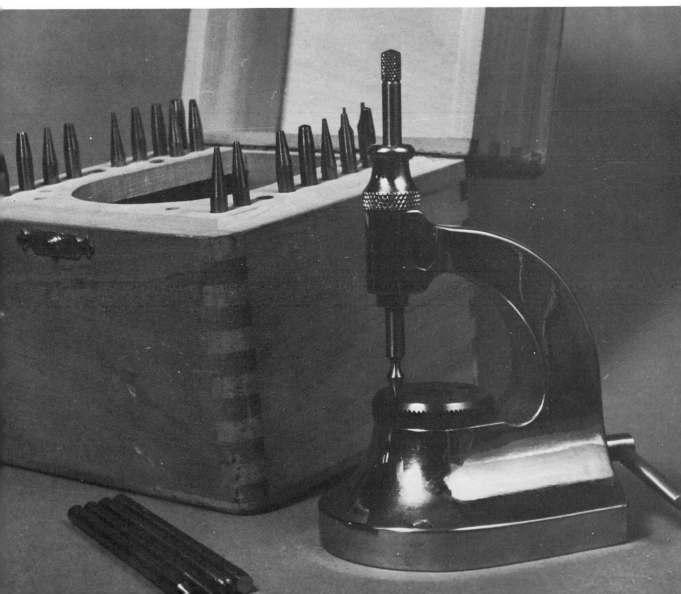

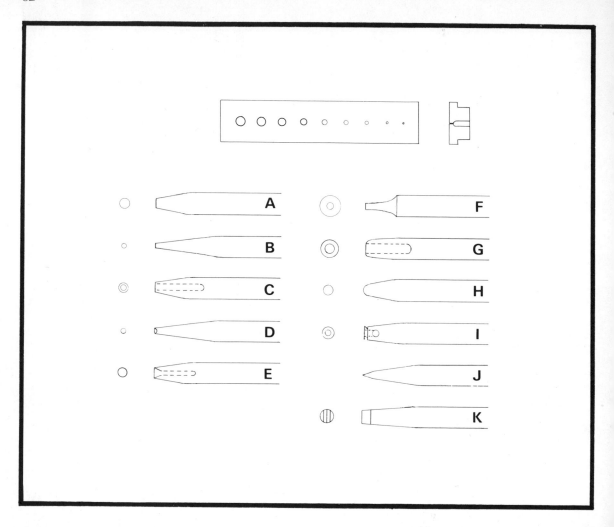

Punches and Stakes.
The steel stake has various holes for supporting work
of different diameters. The narrow holes have a
clearance hole below as shown in the side view and
the lips rest on the top of the jaws of the vice which
grip the body of the stake
[A] Plain punch
[B] Plain punch of smaller diameter
[C] Hollow punch
[D] Punch with hemispherical recess
[E] Hollow punch with sharp edges
[F] Parallel flat ended punch
[G] Rounded hollow punch
[H] Rounded solid punch
[I] Hollow punch with clearance hole
[J], [K] Chisel shaped punches

number of clippings of material which can be
used for wiping off dirt, removing polish etc.
He visited the church and wound the clock in
the tower, checking its accuracy and applying
fresh oil after that which had overflowed had
been wiped away. He examined the pulleys
carrying the weight lines and ensured that the
latter were not showing signs of fraying. A
twelve-inch dial clock in the vestry had also to
be wound and regulated and he then returned
to his midday meal.

His afternoon was spent in dealing with
work that had been brought in by the market
people; a new mainspring in an American
Sharp Gothic striking clock, another thirty-
hour long-case clock which needed cleaning
and rebushing, a further verge watch that

wanted cleaning and a new glass and an American O.G. clock which had fallen from the wall and smashed its glass, broken its weight lines, bent the pendulum and broken the minute hand. A traveller came to take orders for materials such as watch glasses, necklace fastenings and various other small items and spent a short while chatting and giving the latest news from London.

Saturday This day was like Thursday on a smaller scale but after the local factories closed at 4 p.m. the streets became very crowded with people shopping. Two young men who had been members of a watch club and now

Right Sharp Gothic striking clock by Brewster and Ingrahams, Bristol, Conn., U.S.A. About 1850

Below a Turret clock movement of the early 19th century. Movements such as this were found in churches all over the country and were usually maintained by the local clockmaker

had saved enough, came to the shop to purchase watches which they intend shall last them their lifetime and possibly serve the next generation as well. They chose fullplate levers in silver cases after having slowly and deliberately examined most of the watches in stock, and have enough money to purchase white metal Albert chains to go with them. In later years, perhaps, these chains will be changed for something better but their money does not allow anything more elaborate at present. The evening wore on with further customers arriving to bring or collect repairs and it was past 10 o'clock before the shutters could be put up.

Sunday On Sunday no work was ever done. Convention demanded attendance at church and the clockmaker and his wife in their Sunday best, walked to the parish church, gravely greeting various neighbours and business acquaintances on the way. Near the church, they met the town's other watch-maker accompanied by his wife, but as he was 'chapel' and our man was 'church' they passed each other without a nod of recognition. No member of either congregation would have dreamt of patronising the clockmaker who attended the other place of worship. On arrival at the church, the clockmaker looked up at the tower and compared the time shown with that

Fullplate Lever watch in a silver case with chain, about 1850. The seconds dial is not sunk below the level of the main dial

indicated by his watch. If any serious difference were observed he might make an adjustment on the spot in spite of the Sabbath, for everyone in the town knew that he looked after the church clock, and his reputation must be maintained at all cost. It was more than likely that all was in order, for he kept a close watch on the going of the clock every week when he wound it. He left his wife in the porch for a few minutes while he went to the vestry door and looked in to check the going of the vestry clock. All was in order and he returned to his wife and they entered the church for their devotions. The afternoon was spent in resting after a traditional Sunday dinner, and the evening involved another visit to the church and then early to bed.

So proceeded the life of a typical clockmaker in a country town, and there would have been little change until 1914. As the century progressed, the wooden Black Forest clocks would be replaced by spring-driven factory clocks from the same area, the American clocks would increase in number and variety and the French clocks would appear more and more in black marble cases. English watches were increasingly replaced by Swiss or American ones and the end of the century would bring in the first very cheap watches. The metal-cased drum alarm clocks increased in popularity from the 1880s onwards. Similar movements without alarms were fitted in wooden or even marble cases, and a scaled-down version about 2 in. in diameter was popular fitted into china cases. These changes took place slowly and made little impact as they occurred.

The nineteenth century also saw many clocks and watches converted from the verge escapement; the anchor escapement was usually chosen for clocks and the lever escapement for watches. Britten's *Watch and Clockmaker's Handbook* [1884 edition] included a large number of specimen trains for converting verge watches to lever escapement. During this period, a number of old English lantern clocks were also provided with modern spring-driven movements so that they could be used as mantel clocks which was by no means a happy arrangement.

7
MODERN DEVELOPMENTS

The period after 1918 saw a number of important changes in the horological world. The most important was the increased use of the wrist watch. This had first been worn by officers in the German navy about 1911 and the conflict of 1914–18 provided further opportunity for its extended use. It was rapidly established as normal wear for ladies, but it took practically twenty years for it to become really popular among men. Nowadays it is taken so much for granted that waistcoats are less popular than they used to be and the sale of pocket watches is very small indeed, although there has been some attempt to revive interest in them. Few, if any, key-wind watches were made after 1918, but they were still available for sale as late as 1932, being regularly advertised on the Saturday mail order page of the Daily Express.

ELECTRIC CLOCKS

The extension of the electric grid in the 1930s led to the synchronous electric clocks which are still popular. Previously, electric clocks were very scarce in domestic use, the Eureka and the Boulle being the best known. Electric clocks were generally only used in large buildings where a master clock drove a number of slave dials in various rooms. The synchronous movement is now even used for turret clocks although it suffers from the disadvantage of stopping during power cuts. A better method is where the old clock movement is retained and automatically wound at regular intervals by electricity. There is enough reserve of power to keep the clock going for several hours in the event of a power cut. At the present time it is difficult to find people to

wind turret clocks, and the electric winding system is a convenient answer to the problem.

The construction of turret clocks underwent a revolution when the clock for the Houses of Parliament was made by Dent in 1854. The old birdcage frame was abandoned and a flat frame adopted, more like a printing press, together with the double three-legged gravity escapement. This set a new fashion in turret clock movements and not only basically altered manufacturing methods but also made the work of maintenance much easier. A feature of pre-electric clock days was the winding and maintenance contract. Large blocks of offices or hospitals or any buildings where a large number of clocks were in use made a contract with a firm of clockmakers for

A Turret clock by Gillett & Co. 1885. The flat bed construction and gravity escapement are derived from Lord Grimthorpe's design for the clock on the Houses of Parliament (Big Ben) which was made in 1854

Watch cleaning machines. The parts are contained in the wire basket which is dipped into each jar in turn and rotated by the motor. The third jar contains a rinsing solution and the fourth is supplied with warm air for drying

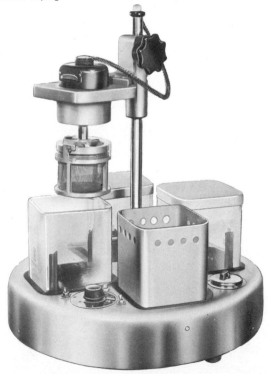

the winding and maintenance of all these clocks, and a representative of the firm attended once a week to do the winding and undertake any on-the-spot repairs that could be accomplished without much bother. Anything more drastic required the removal of the clock to the workshop and probably the loan of a substitute clock until the original one was repaired. Most of the clocks involved would have been English dials with fusees, but the rapid replacement of them by electric clocks, meant that many of these clocks have been scrapped particularly in the period after 1945. A repair to an electric clock usually means the replacement of the movement by a new one.

The railways needed large numbers of clocks for their stations, offices etc., and usually maintained their own workshops where repairs were undertaken. These workshops also undertook repairs and maintenance of the watches issued to the operating staff. These watches had to give a high standard of accuracy and in the early days were mostly English watches with fusees, but later in the nineteenth century various lines used imported watches such as Walthams on the London Brighton and South Coast Railway and Seth Thomas on the Somerset and Dorset Railway. Most of the clocks supplied to the railways were English; the Great Northern patronised Stockall, Marples and the London and the South Western preferred John Walker and Son.

CLEANING AND TIMING ADVANCES

Perhaps the most revolutionary aids to watch repairing are the cleaning machines and the electronic timer. The cleaning machine uses a wire basket which contains the parts of the watch apart from the balance, and rotates it electrically in a cleaning solution. The basket is then raised above the surface of the solution and spun to get rid of the excess fluid, after which it is given the same treatment in a second bath and spun again. A third bath contains rinse and then the basket is filled with warm air to dry the parts. Assembly is undertaken immediately and no further attention is required such as pegging out. Another modern development is the ultrasonic cleaner where the watch is immersed in a special solution and made to vibrate at a very high frequency. The dirt particles are dislodged and carried away by the solution and the watch can then be re-lubricated and set going. Lubricants are being further developed. Formerly a watch could be lubricated with watch oil made from the jaw of a porpoise, but now special oils are made for different parts of the watch and even self-lubricating cleaning agents can be used.

The only way to test a watch in days gone by was to let it run in the shop and compare its performance with the shop regulator; a time-piece with a compensated pendulum and dead-beat escapement that kept a very close rate. Every day the watch would be slightly adjusted until it was keeping time. The new electronic timers listen to the tick of the watch and indicate by marks on a strip of paper whether it is losing or gaining and by approximately how much. An adjustment of the index can be made and its effect immediately noted so a watch can be brought to time within minutes.

THE EBAUCHE SYSTEM

A century ago, a watchmaker needing a new part for a watch would probably have had to make it. Nowadays under the Ebauche system, spare parts are easily obtainable through the post from material dealers and as they are precision made there is no anxiety about their fitting. The 'Ebauche' is the rough movement, i.e. plates, wheels and barrel and Ebauches are made by a group of firms and then sold to many other factories who finish the watches according to their own ideas. Naturally there is not much difference in the finished watches, so spare parts are ordered from a catalogue of Ebauches and movements are identified by examining the front plate under the dial and comparing it with the official Ebauche catalogue to find the correct reference of the movement. Once this is established, the filling in of the order is just routine, and the dealers can despatch the spare parts to the repairers immediately.

Another improvement from the point of view of the maintenance is the unbreakable mainspring. Broken mainsprings usually meant that the watch had to be completely stripped to insert a new one, and in addition the shock of breaking could damage some of the leaves of the centre pinion. Certain American factories got over this difficulty in the previous century by screwing the centre pinion on its arbor, and the kick given to the barrel by the breaking mainspring simply unscrewed the pinion without doing any damage.

SELF-WINDING WATCHES

While the present tendency is towards simplification, the opposite is found in the self-winding watch. Every movement of the wearer's wrist causes a weight inside the watch to rotate and thereby slightly wind the mainspring. This is an advantage not only because the watch never needs winding by hand while it is being worn, but also because in normal use the mainspring tends to keep near the fully wound position and the tension, and therefore the force applied to the train, is more constant than when the spring is allowed to run down completely each day. The winding gear itself needs special care when the watch is being taken down as it contains some tiny gears and ball races.

ELECTRIC WATCHES

In the 1950s the electric watch made its appearance, being driven by a tiny battery about 1 cm. in diameter. The original watches were of the conventional type, relying on the battery only as a substitute for the mainspring, but later watches used a tuning fork as the timekeeping standard, and now watches are made where the time is kept by a vibrating quartz crystal. The accuracy of a quartz crystal watch is estimated to be within one minute per year. These watches are very different from the spring-driven watches of the 1940s and the repairer has had to learn a number of new techniques to keep abreast of latest developments. Many watches now indicate the day of the month, a feature seen as long ago as the seventeenth century, but rare after the early eighteenth. The date mechanism adds to the complication of the watch. A new idea of 1971 has gone back to

Left movement of a mantel clock with Westminster chimes about 1930. Many such movements were made in Germany 1920–39

Below chiming mantel clock about 1930. This example is British but very similar to the ones supplied from Germany

basic principles in design for the watch itself, but the movement is made out of plastic, and as many of the parts are moulded together as units, it contains far fewer parts than the metal watch it replaces. The movement cannot be taken apart and the idea is that when it needs repair it is simply thrown away and replaced by a new one.

FASHIONS IN DOMESTIC CLOCKS

Most of the clocks sold in Britain between the wars were of German origin, and many were made with quarter chimes. They included a device for self-correction if the chimes got out of step with the hands and were very popular, both in the long-case and mantel versions. The maintenance of the movements did not present any great problems and spare parts were easily available. Many of these clocks are now being scrapped as the present fashion is for smaller clocks, and chimes and even hour striking are becoming less fashionable. More and more people rely solely on their wrist watches for the time. At present, smaller clocks are still made which are driven by springs but versions have been produced that hang on the wall and are wound by pulling a cord. Many clocks of today are battery-driven and require new techniques in their repair.

In spite of all these developments, certain traditions are still maintained. The well known

Above clockmaker's lathe operated by treadle. About 1860

Below watch fusees and barrels. On the left from a Verge watch; on the right, unfinished examples intended for a Lever watch which is thinner

Black Forest cuckoo clock is still being produced in its old form with weight-drive, although some movements are sophisticated enough to have rack striking in place of the countwheel, and some are provided with an ingenious kick-starting device for releasing the strike. These clocks, of course, have to be dealt with by a repairer, but ultrasonic cleaning reduces the time spent on them. Many factories on the Continent are turning out reproductions of old styles, one Italian model even having the short 'cowtail' pendulum swinging before the dial, while wall clocks are being produced in Black Forest factories which have an affinity with the old Black Forest wall clocks of the early nineteenth century.

Many magazines devoted to furnishings illustrate rooms decorated in the most modern style but containing an old clock such as an English dial. The price of old clocks of types which were considered quite ordinary a few years ago has risen alarmingly in the last few years and indicates their popularity. While the interest in these old clocks is maintained, repairers will be needed to deal with them, and there is a scarcity of skilled labour at the moment which means that all shops are extremely busy. The craft of the clockmaker is not yet dead.

A few accessories: the brass and steel tweezers are used for picking up small parts, oilstone powder gives a polish to steel. Rottenstone mixed with oil is used for cleaning brass, pith is used for removing cleaning and polishing agents after the work is clean and pegwood is used for cleaning pivot holes in plates, by sharpening to a point, inserting, rotating and resharpening until the pegwood emerges spotless. The eyeglass for examining small parts is made of horn

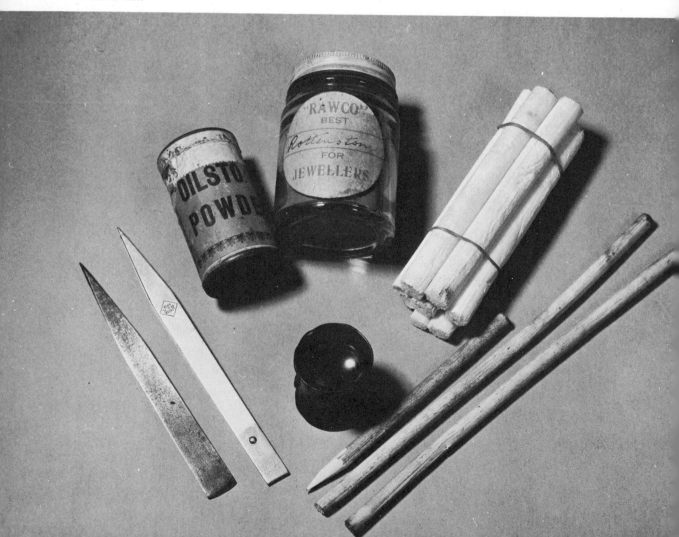

APPENDIX I

As an illustration that R. Blakeborough of Otley was not unique in carrying on a business in addition to that of watch and clockmaker, the following list has been compiled of additional trades carried on by horologists. The majority of them have been extracted from 'Yorkshire Clockmakers' by Brian Loomes, and the others from early 19th century directories.

Baker, Confectioner, Printer, Flour Dealer, Umbrella Maker, Furniture Broker, Ironmonger, Tea Dealer, Toy Seller, Dealer in Glass and China, Hardware Dealer, Spirit Merchant, Victualler, Cut Glass Dealer, Day School Teacher, Postmaster, Grocer and Draper.

APPENDIX II

In order to show the amount of subdivision of labour in the horological trade, the following list of separate occupations has been compiled from the Post Office London Directory of 1846.

Clock Maker, Clock Case Maker, Clock Glass Maker, Clock Tool Maker, Watch Cap Maker, Watch Case Maker, Watch Dial Plate Maker and Finisher, Watch and Clock Dial Silverer, Watch Enameller, Watch Engine Turner, Watch Engraver, Watch Escapement Maker, Watch Finisher, Watch Fusee Maker, Watch Case Gilder, Watch and Clock Glass Maker, Watch Hand Maker, Watch Index Maker, Watch Jeweller, Watch Joint Finisher, Watch Key Maker, Watch Material Dealer, Watch Motion Maker, Watch Pallet Jeweller, Watch Pallet Maker, Watch Pendant Maker, Watch Pinion Maker, Watch Secret Springer, Watch Spring Maker, Watch and Clock Tool Maker and Dealer, Watch Wheel Maker and Watch Maker.

APPENDIX III

A short list of museums possessing clockmakers' tools.

British Isles

Basingstoke, Hants. (Willis Museum)	Small collection of tools.
Braintree, Essex	Wheel-cutting engine belonging to the Fordham family.
Broadway, Glos. (National Trust, Snowshill Manor)	Wheel-cutting engines, lathe and hammers.
Christchurch, Hants. (Red House Museum)	Fusee chain tools.
Colchester, Essex	Wheel-cutting engine belonging to the Hedge family of Colchester.
Haworth, Yorks. (Brontë Museum)	Wheel used by the local clockmaker, Barraclough, for driving his throw.
Huddersfield, Yorks. (Tolson Memorial Museum)	Workshop with a fair selection of tools.
Leicester (Newarke Houses Museum)	The complete workshop of Samuel Deacon, Barton-in-the-Beans.
Liverpool, Lancs. (City of Liverpool Museum)	Collection of tools.
London (British Museum)	A few tools in the Students' Room. View by appointment only.
(Science Museum)	Wheel-cutting engines, lathes and fusee engines in the Machine Tool section.
Oxford (Museum of the History of Science)	Clock-wheel engine, balance-wheel engine.
Norwich, Norfolk (Bridewell Museum)	Small collection of tools.
St. Fagans, Glamorgan (National Museum of Wales)	Wheel engines and lathe.
Truro, Cornwall (County Museum)	Wheel-cutting engines.

Overseas

Denmark	*Aarhus* (Den Gamle By)	Small collection of tools.
France	*Besançon*	A new horological display is being planned. Tools may be included.
Germany	*Augsburg* (Maximilian Museum)	Wheel-cutting engines, lathe, fusee cutter.
	Furtwangen (Uhrenmuseum)	Black Forest workshop.
	Munich (Deutsches Museum)	Black Forest workshop.
	Neustadt (Heimatstuben)	Black Forest workshop.
	Schwenningen (Heimatmuseum)	Black Forest workshop and other tools on display.
	(Kienzle Museum)	Wheel-cutting engine, mandrel, turns, depthing tool, rounding-up tool and uprighting tool.
Netherlands	*Leeuwarden* (Fries Museum)	Small collection of tools usually kept in a house some distance away and not generally on display.
	Utrecht (Klokkenmuseum)	Various tools included in the collection.
Switzerland	*La Chaux de Fonds*	A new museum of horology is being planned and tools will probably be included.
	Winterthur (Old Town Hall, Kellenberger Collection)	Turns, bow, drills, wheel engine and etc.
United States	*Bristol, Connecticut* (American Clock and Watch Museum)	Wheel engine and various tools for wooden movements.
	(Connecticut Historical Society)	Burnap tools, can be viewed on application to Curator.
	Greenfield Village, Michigan (Henry Ford Museum)	Watch and clock tools.
	Washington, DC. (Smithsonian Institution)	Tools for wooden movements.
	Winterthur, Delaware (Winterthur Museum)	Collection of tools.

BIBLIOGRAPHY

Bailey, F. A.
and Barker, T. C. — *The Seventeenth Century Origins of Watchmaking in West Lancashire, Liverpool and Merseyside.*

Beeson, C. F. C. — *English Church Clocks 1280–1850* [Antiquarian Horological Society 1971].

Britten, F. J. — *Watch and Clockmaker's Handbook, Dictionary and Guide* [Various editions 1878 onwards. E. & F. N. Spon].

Clutton C. — *The Performance of Early Watches* [Antiquarian Horology Supplement December 1954. Antiquarian Horological Society.]

Daniels, George — *English and American Watches* [Abelard Schuman 1967].

De Carle, Donald — *Practical Clock Repairing* [N.A.G. Press 2nd Edition 1968].
Practical Watch Repairing [N.A.G. Press 1946].
The Watchmaker's Lathe [Robert Hale & Co. 1971].

Dinsdale, Rev. N. V. — *The Old Clockmakers of Yorkshire* [The Yorkshire Dalesman 1946].

Garrard, F. J. — *Clock Repairing and Making* [Crosby Lockwood].
Watch Repairing, Cleaning and Adjusting [Crosby Lockwood 1928].

Gazeley, W. J. — *Watch and Clock Making and Repairing* [Heywood & Company Ltd. 1953].

Gilbert, K. R. — *The Machine Tool Collection* [Science Museum Catalogue of Exhibits H.M.S.O. 1966].

Gordon, G. F. C. — *Clockmaking Past and Present* [The Technical Press 1946].

Hasluck, Paul N. — *The Clock Jobber's Handybook* [Crosby Lockwood 1881 and subsequently].
The Watch Jobber's Handybook [Crosby Lockwood 1881 and subsequently].

Hoopes, Penrose R. — *The Shop Records of Daniel Burnap, Clockmaker* [Connecticut Historical Society 1958].

Loomes, Brian — *Yorkshire Clockmakers* [Dalesman Books 1972].

Masters, John Neve — *Amusing Reminiscences of Victorian Times and Today* [Published by Author 1921].

Mühe, R. — *Die Historische Uhrensammlung* [Furtwangen 1967. Revised 1972 under the title *Uhren und Zeitmessung*].

Ottema, Nanne — *Geschiedenis van de Uurwermakerskunst in Friesland* [Van Gorcum & Co. N. V. Assen 1948].

Peate, Iorwerth C. — *Clock and Watch Makers in Wales* [National Museum of Wales 1960].

Rees, Abraham — *Clocks, Watches and Chronometers*]David and Charles 1970].

Roberts, Kenneth D. (Ed.) — *American Waltham Watch Co. 1885* [Trade Catalog with Price List].
American Watch Co., Waltham, Mass. [New Orleans Exposition 1884–5].
Elgin Reminiscences. Making Watches by Machinery 1869.
(Three Reprints by Ken Roberts Publishing Co., Bristol, Conn. 1972.)

Saunier, Claudius — *The Watch Maker's Handbook* [Crosby Lockwood 1888].

Symonds, R. W. — *Thomas Tompion, His Life and Work* [Batsford 1951].

Thiout, Antoine — *Traité de l'Horlogerie* [Editions du Palais Royal, Paris 1972].

White, Allen — *The Chain Makers—A History of the Watch Fusee Chain Industry* [Published by author 1967].

Wilding, John — *A Weight-driven Eight-Day Wall Clock* [Brant Wright, Ashford, Kent 1972].
How to Make a Weight-driven 8-day Wall Clock [Horological Journal, Ashford, Kent].

INDEX